Letters from Section 17

A Collection of *Morningside* Essays

Fred McGuinness

GREAT PLAINS
PUBLICATIONS

Great Plains Publications
3—161 Stafford Street
Winnipeg, Manitoba
R3M 2X9

The publisher acknowledges the financial assistance of The Canada Council and the Manitoba Arts Council in the production of this book.

Design & Typography by Taylor George Design
Printed in Canada by Friesens

CANADIAN CATALOGUING IN PUBLICATION DATA

McGuinness, Fred
Letters from Section 17 : a collection of Morningside essays

ISBN 1-894283-07-4
1 Country life—Prairie Provinces 2. Prairie Provinces—Social life and customs. I. Morningside (Radio program). II. Title

FC3237.M27 1999 971.2 C99-920177-8
F1060.M138 1999

For Christine

Contents

Foreword

FOR ALMOST 60 YEARS, FRED MCGUINNESS HAS COMMITTED HIS UNIQUE talents of communication to the understanding, appreciation and celebration of life in rural western Canada. His accomplishments have been extraordinary and in the course of his remarkable career in popular journalism he has earned the genuine esteem and affection of the many people whose lives he has touched. This book contains reflections and 'anecdotage' (a McGuinnessism) drawn from a life rich in memories.

While some of the pieces recall family life, most are drawn from experiences gained as a journalist, executive director of the Saskatchewan Jubilee, or as editor and publisher of the newspapers in the West. All were written and delivered in Fred's inimitable voice and style on Peter Gzowski's CBC *Morningside* program.

Fred McGuinness is a gifted storyteller. Each of these recollections reflects Fred's deep curiosity about life around him, his enviable ability to find the humour in every situation, and his unique ability to convey action, ideas and nuance directly and concretely. All reflect the sensibility of a man who enjoys life, appreciates characters, and possesses a rare talent for filing away memorable experiences for future reference.

A few years ago when Fred received an honorary doctoral degree from Brandon University, the University received many letters celebrating his life and accomplishments. One writer characterized Fred as the undisputed Dean of community newspaper editors and journalists. He was, asserted another, "a philosopher, a lecturer, a specialist in arborculture (especially of the Christmas tree variety), a protector of grammatical English, an advisor generous with his time, and on top of it all, a mighty fine gentleman." He was celebrated as "the ultimate rural life enthusiast."

All of these qualities are reflected in the contents of this book. Most of all, readers will discover a veritable cornucopia of warmth, wisdom and prairie erudition. It will put a grin on your face from one cover to another and rekindle your appreciation for the fine art of story telling, for in these pages you are in the hands of a master.

Tom Mitchell
McKee Archives, BRANDON UNIVERSITY

Introduction

OVER THE PAST 60 YEARS IT HAS BEEN MY GOOD FORTUNE TO WORK IN close association with interesting individuals. These were great learning experiences: railway, navy, boarding school, university, and then that people-filled world of journalism.

Thousands of the tiny encounters between humans were memorable. Even before I knew you could write for money, I was recording these incidents for my own pleasure. The result is that they are safely stored in my memory box.

I call them anecdotes. Indeed, I refer to them so frequently that my daughter Colleen insists that I am in my anecdotage. They would have remained strictly confidential had not Peter Gzowski given me a dream assignment; the opportunity to be the rural commentator on his CBC radio show *Morningside*. Peter's instructions were specific: I could write about anything I wished as long as it wasn't a political commentary.

Now that I can look back on this rich experience, there are persons who must be recognized. First, Peter, for his trust and patience. Standing right beside him is a remarkable woman known simply as "The Countess." My contact for *Morningside* was Shelley Ambrose. When I asked her what she liked to be called;

I gave her some options: Miss, Mrs. Ms., Dr., Prof., among others. She said she had always favoured the name Countess, and Countess Ambrose she became. She turned work into fun.

On the home front is someone worthy of extraspecial recognition. My loving partner of 50 years plus is Christine, an artist with the articles of punctuation. Week after month over a dozen years she edited my *Morningside* copy and delivered opinions, occasionally with a smile, sometimes with a frown, but always with the commas and semicolons exactly where they should be. Profound thanks.

Nor can I forget Gregg Shilliday, publisher of Great Plains Publications. He had the vision to see that there was another life for the "Letters from Section 17" and this book is the result.

Boyhood

CP Telegraphs.

"HEY, FREDDIE, PUT ON YOUR TIN PANTS." WHEN ART CARR CALLED OUT this strange instruction his face was wreathed in smiles. At the same time the two other telegram messengers on duty, Murray McKay and Harry Mummery, hooted in laughter. I had been on the CPR payroll only a couple of weeks at this time and I was still learning about embedded secrets in the corporate culture; perhaps this was one of them. I took that telegram from the operator, put it in an envelope, and marched forth.

It was to be delivered only a short distance from the office, and so I walked. As I did I pondered that strange instruction, and the gales of laughter it evoked. I made my way up to the second floor of a building on Rosser Avenue in Brandon and pushed my way through an office door.

Well, I was greeted by the original Mr. Friendly. He wanted to know my name, where I lived, how long I'd been a messenger—it was quite a quiz. Impressed as I was by his obviously caring attitude, I answered in detail.

When it came time for me to make my delivery, he didn't want the message pushed across the counter, rather he wanted to come around to my side. He took the envelope. He signed the book. He put his left arm around my shoulders as if to signify that we were friends for life, and while I thought this unusual, I didn't twig to anything until I realized what he was doing with his right hand; he had undone my fly buttons and was fishing inside.

This was my introduction to "The Menace." Every messenger in the service had been through the same experience. While we were unanimous in our loathing of the man there wasn't much we could do about it: if a telegram came in for his company, we were expected to deliver it. In my case I devised my own plan: if there was anyone else in that office

I would go through the standard routine. If The Menace was alone, I dropped the message on the counter and hurried away. On my way back to the office I fudged his signature on the allotted line.

In my two years as "boy with wheel," this is the only unpleasant memory I can recall. The work certainly was interesting; the crew was friendly; the customers were always courteous. Really, there was only one problem; the pay was lamentable. Twenty-nine dollars a month is not the avenue to riches, but in 1935 it was the going rate for those on the lowest rung of the ladder.

Once I gravitated to the evening shift, I learned that our work came in batches. We would have a busy spell, invariably followed by hours of boredom. By this time I had decided that I could become an operator and so I began to practice. Art Carr wrote out the code for me, and in my idle hours I undertook my self-applied training.

I always used the way-wires, those being the telegraph lines that ran parallel to the branch rail lines. I did so because they were almost always silent in the evenings. As message material I used the pages of the *Brandon Sun* and night after night station agents (they used to live in the depots) in villages like Neudorf and Napinka could hear my fumbling efforts to transmit the stories of the day.

I can bring some of them to mind: Rhoda Tennant became Brandon's first female councillor; ex-Lieutenant-Governor J.D. McGregor died three years after dedicating Riding Mountain National Park; residents of the North end are in revolt; they claim (rightly as it turned out) that a proposed bridge over the CPR tracks would trespass upon their land; the dogcatcher was mauled by a German shepherd.

Over the months I knew I was making progress, and the proof positive came on the night when I left the telegraph key shut for a few minutes and the sounder began to clatter:

I recognized the first word: H-E-L-L-O. This was followed ever so slowly by still more words, "W-H-O A-R-E Y-O-U A-N-D W-H-E-R-E A-R-E Y-O-U."

Breakthrough! For a second at least I felt like a combination Bell-Marconi when those giants heard the first words on their marvelous inventions. Ever so quickly (but slowly) I replied with my name, and the name of my town, and explained that I certainly would appreciate a buddy with whom to practice.

It may surprise you if I say that true love can spring sight unseen from a casual conversation, but I had a standard 15-year-old's imagination and it began to work overtime. After all, I now had this regular connection. Brenda, the daughter of the station agent at Wellwood, wanted to become my constant evening companion. As we became more proficient with the Morse I learned that she was a student, that she came to Brandon occasionally, and yes, she would like to meet me.

I looked up Wellwood on the railway map: Rats! It was 40 miles distant, too far to reach via cycle. I became terribly impatient with the CPR on those rare occasions, like election day, or the day of a hockey game, when we were extra busy; this meant that Brenda and I would have to forego our evening tryst.

What burst my bubble and introduced me to the world of knavery was the night Art Carr had had enough of my mooning over the telegraph key. "You're a dizzy young bugger," he said, in what I thought was an indelicate outburst. "You're being put on. There is no Brenda. There's only an assistant station agent at Wellwood and he has nothing to do until the next train comes through. He's as bad as you are!" At that point—a little older and a lot wiser—I fell out of love with someone I had never met.

Another unusual experience occurred one afternoon when I was parking my bike by the front door. A voice behind me said, "P-s-s-t, kid: do you want to make a dollar?" That's like asking if birds care to fly.

Ever so carefully I listened to the requirements. I was to go into the telegraph office and call the Yard Office. Once they answered I was to ask for the whereabouts of Trainman X. I was to copy down the answer because I had to have it right.

I did as instructed. The clerk in the Yard Office obviously looked something up in his documents because he was specific: "Trainman X left Brandon at eleven hundred hours on a freight train headed for Broadview. The earliest he can be back here is tomorrow afternoon, on another freight."

I nipped out to the street and whispered this news to my benefactor. He then asked me to write a message, put it in an envelope, and deliver it promptly. The message read, "Waiting for you in room 17, Cecil Hotel." There was no signature. I did as bid, making my delivery to a woman who lived in the west end. Later that day when I saw her on the street, westward bound, I thought she looked real sexy. Every time this story comes to mind I think I should write a book, "I Was A Pimp For The CPR."

Writing out that message reminds me of some of the strange wordings we saw as persons attempted to keep within the 10-word confines of a full-rate telegram. Operator Agnes Bartlett copied a message one day and gave it to me to put in an envelope for delivery. It read: "PASSING THROUGH TODAY TRAIN FOUR MEET ME WITH 44 ROSES." The man to whom I delivered it opened it and cursed roundly: he asked me, "What kind of a dumb bastard has a need for 44 roses in a railway compartment?"

Plumbing the depths of my 15-year wisdom, I offered an opinion. I suggested that perhaps there was an alternative. Could it be that what the man on the train wanted was a forty-ounce bottle of Four Roses whiskey? For my cunning decoding of this cryptic message I received a one-dollar tip, at that time a day's pay. I've often wondered what kind of a reception he would have had if he had shown up at the train with a florist's box under each arm.

Messenger Murray McKay put his name in the (unofficial) Guinness Book of Records the day he fell off his bike. Murray kept his false teeth in his back pocket when he was out in the really cold weather. One noon hour, his front wheel caught in the streetcar tracks and down he went, landing on his teeth. They shattered, and a shard gave him a puncture wound which required medical attention. He didn't think it at all funny when the rest of us proclaimed him the first person in the history of the Wheat City to bite himself on the ass.

The Button Bag

MANY, MANY YEARS AGO, IN THOSE PRE-TV, EVEN PRE-RADIO DAYS, WHEN my little sisters and I tired of playing Parcheesi, or Snakes and Ladders, we would get out an unusual household item that gave us countless hours of pleasure.

It was the button bag. It hung on the inside knob of the dining-room door. It was almost as large as a rugby ball. It was made of flax-colored linen, with drawstring top. Its sides were decorated with a repeating pattern of pansies executed in cross-stitch.

One of us would carry it to the dining-room table, where we made a fence of flesh with our arms as we dumped it out.

Now, this wasn't just a bag filled with buttons; this was a lifetime assembly of buttons and other small memorabilia. My mother had worked on this collection from the days of the family homestead at 22:15:02, west of the second meridian.

Frugality was the order of the day on the agricultural frontier, so no small artifact was ever thrown away. You just knew that if you kept something seven years you'd find a second use for it.

In those early days, every time you discarded an article of clothing you stripped it of every button, clasp, and dome fastener.

We first paired up all the buttons, and this was quite an assignment. We had them in the hundreds. There were buttons plain, and buttons coloured. There were buttons with two holes, and three holes, and four.

There were leather buttons, wooden buttons, even toggles from early versions of the parka. There were fancy buttons galore, snipped from ball gowns dated from the turn of the century, perhaps even earlier.

With all the buttons organized, it now was time for the memorabilia. At this point the scene changes from the oddments collected by a needlewoman to the very stuff of social history.

We lined up the military badges so neatly they made us think of soldiers on the parade square.

Uncle Fred had been a doctor in the Royal Canadian Medical Corps, and we had his tunic buttons and one hat badge. These were easy to identify; they had the serpents of Aesculapius entwined on a wand, although we didn't understand this at the time.

We had buttons and badges that belonged to Uncle George. He was a soldier in the 181st Battalion, and he died at Vimy Ridge. A man who later worked in the Brandon post office had been with him when he lost his life. He had clipped two buttons off Uncle's tunic, and given them to his mother.

Uncle Roy was a youthful bandsman and we had buttons from his uniform. This was heroic stuff. First he was mentioned in dispatches, and later awarded the Military Medal. He ran for help through enemy lines when a small company of men was cut off from the rest of the battalion. We even had that tiny piece of striped fabric that designated his medal. The medal itself was in safekeeping in a bureau drawer, and we were not allowed to touch that.

When a real collector sets out to store away the memorabilia of a lifetime, there is no end to the variety.

There was a little nickel (can you remember them?) slightly bent and highly polished. One day on the homestead my mother had found it in the gizzard of the Christmas turkey.

There were tourist souvenirs from Gananoque where my grandparents settled briefly on their arrival from Ireland.

There was a handful of coins, and we knew the story behind each of them. These were *zlotys*, and *pfennigs*, and some German coins with a story all their own. Uncle Harry had traded them away from a German soldier on Christmas Day when the warriors in the trenches got tired of killing each other and spent the day fraternizing.

There was a collection of thimbles, also from the homestead. Some of them were heavily scarred by work needles.

From what my mother told us, her mother could sew anything: clothing, binder canvas, even the hides of cattle that had been gored.

Now, I suspect that I will be greeted with disbelief if I try to tell the story of the button bag to some grandchild engaged with Nintendo, but this doesn't matter.

It's a precious memory to me. When I went home for mother's funeral I looked behind the dining-room door—no button bag. One of my sisters got there first.

Christmas Tales

Let me give you my view of the festive season: for the young, it's a time of gifts; for the old, it's a time of memories.

From my boyhood home I recall the air of what I must call feverish secrecy. Conversations ceased abruptly if a young one wandered into a room where adults were speaking. There were a lot of whispered telephone conversations in that week before Christmas.

Oh yes, one thing more: anyone caught shaking or rattling the presents under the tree was due for a scolding. In the late '20s and early '30s, the festive season was marked by a blizzard of cards... Christmas cards by the hundreds. Cards were a hot topic in the McGuinness household because we had a postman who always drank too much. When he was offered a Christmas drink, he was too polite to say no. He was often potted by the time he got to our place.

No matter his condition, this faithful courier was determined that every home on his route was going to get some mail.

I can remember the THUMP!! as he dropped the mail on the floor of the porch. Some was ours, but also there would be mail for: Corness, Shaw, Buckingham, Kerr... and I can go on with other names of neighbours, sixty years ago.

When I delivered this stuff, I would pick up McGuinness mail which also had been mis-delivered.

Sixty years ago the church was Action Central at the time of Christmas. There were special services. There were concerts, cantatas and other musical evenings.

It was mandatory that every element of church life: cubs, brownies, scouts, guides, young people's club, junior choir, senior choir have a Christmas party, which involved a meal. Each of these consisted of ham, and scalloped potatoes, and your choice of pie.

With six children in our household, we always had someone in every group. Two or three times a week I would deliver a Pyrex bowl of scalloped potatoes to the church kitchen.

Christmas Day began with a trip to church. Many of the parishioners were slightly groggy from lack of sleep: they were the hardy ones who arose at five a.m. to hear Her Majesty's Christmas greetings. In those early times, along with your attachment to the church, there was a stated loyalty to royalty.

When we lived in Regina we had a couple of memorable Christmas seasons. They always come to mind this time of year.

One December 24 the power went off, late in the afternoon. In our home, on Leopold Crescent, we had a fireplace and we had lots of wood, so we knew we wouldn't freeze to death.

The four youngsters thought it was a great treat to have an evening meal of wieners they roasted in the fire. They thought it a great treat to be bathed with candles on the edge of the tub. In the kitchen, however, Christine, (also known as the Queen of Cuisine) did not think it a great treat to stuff the turkey—also by candlelight.

(By the way, because of this experience, we've had a fireplace in every home since.)

Here's one more Christmas memory from a later period. In Medicine Hat, my wife Christine was a member of a sorority, composed mainly of young mothers. When this group heard from the welfare department of a family in great need, they sprang into action.

Because we had a station wagon, Christine and I were the pick-up crew. What we picked up was a full load: I can remember a layette for the new baby, toys and clothing for the children, and a food hamper with all the ingredients for a good Christmas dinner.

This family had a number of children. One of them was a two-year-old who ran around bare naked. We certainly felt rewarded that we could help someone, but we were deeply puzzled that an entire family could arrive in town in Christmas week with no clothing, no furniture, and no money.

There's a happier story from Medicine Hat, it concerns our three sons. One Christmas Santa brought them a table-top hockey game, which they played by the endless hour. Strangely enough, they couldn't get into the spirit unless they were dressed in full hockey gear: helmets, sweaters and shoulder pads.

I have another memory from Medicine Hat, this one arising from my membership in the Rotary Club. Each Christmas, we members took turns ringing the bell for the Salvation Army Christmas Fund.

One Saturday I was on duty in front of the liquor store, ringing away, cajoling the passersby into donating quarters, halves, even the occasional dollar.

I was hard at it when one of my friends came out of the store, bearing a gallon jug of wine. I pressed him hard for a donation. In order to get into his pocket, he put the jug under his left arm, and you can guess what happened.

It slipped. It smashed. The sidewalk was awash with red stuff. Also red was the face of the man who dropped his precious load.

I refuse to tell you what he suggested Santa should do...

Christmas customs are still changing. Each year we hear of more families who are reducing their gift-giving; some of them draw names out of a hat, and it's your responsibility to buy a gift for the person whose name you drew.

When I had my old *Neighbourly News* broadcast, I once wrote about brothers-in-law in Saskatchewan who always exchanged $10,000 cheques on Christmas Day. I call that living dangerously.

And now I must depart. I'm often tardy getting into the spirit, and this tardiness evolves into a blind panic about the 23rd of the month.

There it is now! I feel the spirit coming on!

Carrier #5

One morning, in the early 1970s, I got off the CPR train in Brandon and went for a particular stroll. I had often thought about it, and now I was going to do it: I was going to retrace the path I followed in 1933—'34 as Carrier #5 for the daily newspaper, the *Brandon Sun.*

To me, that carrier route had been a great learning experience. My deliveries covered the heart of the business district. The first was at the Dill Cafe, a most unsavory place right across from the railway tracks. It not only served meals, but it also had rooms to rent on the second floor. The sign said they were available by the day, week, or month. Rumour had it they were available as well by the hour.

As I was only twelve at the time, I was not aware of the local belief that in this enterprise, the waitresses laid the tables on the first floor, and the customers on the second.

From rumoured debauchery to pious rectitude was only half a block: my second customer was the best-known citizen in the territory: Albert Edward McKenzie. He was known universally as just "A.E." He not only founded McKenzie Seeds, the largest seedhouse in the British Empire, but he ruled over his fiefdom until he was 94. Rumours about "A.E." abounded, and I believed none of them. To me, he was a real gentleman.

I delivered a paper at an implement house, and often watched as workers attached cleats to those old-fashioned steel wheels on early-model tractors. I nipped in and out of the poolroom next door ever so quickly, because my mother had taught me that this was the house of the Devil.

The next call was so interesting I could have stayed all day. William Lacey, of Brandon Signs, was a British-taught sign painter. One of his regular customers was the Strand Theatre. For the twice-weekly motion-picture changes, Mr. Lacey painted tall thin signs, about 14 inches wide and four feet deep. These stood behind glass on either side of the theatre entrance.

It intrigued me how he captured the mood of the movie with his artistry. If it was a Lon Chaney spooker, it would show ghostly faces and tombstones. If it was a musical, it would be complete with trombones and the treble clef. When he had finished his lettering, the artist would then paint some glue over selected portions, and cover them with stuff that sparkled.

Two doors later there was a barber shop, and I hated this place so much I had to force myself to enter. The barber had a foul mouth. I went in there one day and a policeman told me I had just lost a customer; the barber was in jail for molesting boys. That was the day I learned two things: that there was a word "buggery" and that it was an indictable offense.

My one bulk sale was five copies to the cigar counter at the Prince Edward Hotel. Then I crossed Ninth Street for another hateful experience.

I had two papers to deliver at the old city hall. One was to the janitor, but the second was at the Relief Office. There were always petitioners at the counter, and they were frequently in tears. The relief officer had a heart of granite. He yelled at people. He wanted every petitioner to exhaust every asset before he would help them. He treated them as if he believed they had gold bars in the mattress.

Then I delivered a paper to the home of a physician, Dr. Peters. His son, Doug, is now Secretary of State for Small Business. His daughter Jean, married Max Freedman. If you are really long in the tooth, you may recall when Max Freedman gave us a commentary from Washington every Sunday noon in an early radio broadcast.

I had plenty of customers on my route, eighty in all, and my deliveries ended at a terrible tenement that could be the subject of a novel by Charles Dickens.

The Imperial Apartments were on the second and third floors over a retail store. There was one toilet per floor, and no tubs. I had perhaps 10 customers in there. Two I remember in particular.

I always pushed a newspaper under one door, and rattled it a bit, and a cheery three-year-old on the other side would pull it all the way through. Occasionally she would open the door and chat with me. There was another doorway that always opened for me, as if my arrival was anticipated: this was an elderly woman who usually had a cookie for me.

I remember these two customers with great sorrow. That three-year-old one day backed into a tub of wash water, and was scalded to death. Later on, I was going to deliver a card to that elderly customer, to mark her 80th birthday. But when I started up the stairs to deliver it, I saw the undertaker's men carrying their basket down. She had died that day. A few years later, when I was home on leave from the navy, I saw that card in a bureau drawer.

Well, one day I wrote a memoir of my newspaper delivery days, and it was published by *Reader's Digest*. It was translated into a dozen different languages. For some months afterward, Brandon expatriates from China, Brazil, Portugal, and other countries sent foreign-language copies home to the Brandon City Hall.

It took me a while to recall why these boyhood memories were so pronounced, and then I reached a conclusion. That paper route covered all the bases: it introduced me to the rich, the poor, the caring, and the despicable.

Come to think of it, that was a great introduction to life.

Early Radio

THE FIRST RADIO ARRIVED IN OUR HOME ABOUT 1929. IT WAS SHAPED like a small window box. It was about a foot high, a foot wide, and around four feet in length. There was no casing and the vacuum tubes glowed like low-power light bulbs. It was called a something Superhetrodyne.

It was powered by a battery, which periodically went to the service station for charging. Only one person listened at a time because earphones were required. We could get signals from two stations: CKY in Winnipeg, and KFYR in Bismarck, North Dakota. Let's say this one was not a conspicuous success.

The next unit, a Philco, required two men to carry it into the living room. The technical workings were housed in a mahogany cabinet which stood about five feet in height. Now we had some listening power.

All those old call letters are still with me. On a crisp winter's night we could get: WCCO Des Moines; WBBM Chicago; KSL Salt Lake City; and there were others.

When I was in about grade three, a friend gave me a crystal set. With a mini-antenna I could get several signals. I would awaken in the morning with a terrible crick in my neck; this is what happens when you fall asleep wearing large, old-fashioned earphones.

There was a period in the mid-'30s in which it was radio signals from the U.S. that gave shape to our day. We could march around the table with Don McNeill and his Breakfast Club. There was a noon-hour farm show, from Chicago. In the evening there was a steady run of major shows like *Major Bowes, The Shadow, and The Lux Radio Theatre.*

In case you wonder how come all this U.S. influence, there is a substantial reason: in those days the predecessor of the CBC broadcast for only a few hours each day.

The advent of the afternoon network brought with it the "soaps," as they were called: Big Sister, Ma Perkins, Pepper Young's Family, and another one I cannot recall. It may have been "The Guiding Light."

Oh yes, this mention of the soaps calls for a digression. Not that many years ago I was in Toronto at a convention. One day when our sessions ended early, I returned to my room in the Westbury. As I approached my room, I could see that the door was open. H-m-m-m.

I peeked in. The chambermaid was seated on the end of the bed, Kleenexes in both hands, tears streaming down her face. I enquired. One of her favourite characters had just died. The soaps may have moved over to TV, but their power - for better or for worse—has not diminished.

In 1928 Brandon had a radio station, CKX, owned and operated by the telephone company. The broadcast content was not to the public favour, and in 1934 the station was bought by James. B. Craig, whose son and grandsons now use it as the foundation of a growing electronic media empire.

But back to my history lesson. I can recall when the Canadian radio listener required a license. My father, once a year, would go to the post office and get one for the price of $1. This entitled him—and his—to listen to the radio for a year.

There were radio police in every community. I can remember them in Brandon, walking up and down the backlanes. If they could see a hank of copper wire coming out of a window—aha—they knew for a certainty that was an antenna—and they demanded to see proof that the one-dollar tariff had been paid.

Among my memorabilia is a notice, signed by A.J. Johnson, deputy minister, Department of Marine and Fisheries. The first paragraph reads: "Owners of unlicensed radio receiving sets are hereby warned that on and after 1st July, 1924, the Department of Marine and Fisheries will take steps to seize any such unlicensed apparatus and to prosecute the owner thereof. The penalty on summary conviction is a fine not exceeding $50.00, and forfeiture of all unlicensed radio apparatus by the Government." Believe me—that didn't last too long.

In 1941, when I came back from the navy, I was convalescing in Deer Lodge Hospital in Winnipeg, and my family gave me the first portable radio I had ever seen. It was about the size of an extra-large brick.

It had good sound, and picked up signals over a fair range, but there was a serious flaw: it was a battery hog. The owner of this portable needed batteries by the case.

In those early times when we young ones were serious readers of comics, we would laugh at Dick Tracy. You may recall that this man had a two-way radio on his wrist.

Well, I don't have one of those—yet. There are a dozen radios in our home, including two in the study in which this column is being written. How's that for lazy: one on each side of the room.

At one time some of us feared that radio would die, a victim of burgeoning TV. This did not occur. Radio is coming on strong. We have more signals. We have specialty stations: sports, news, classics, ethnic, country-western, and there are others. If, some night, I find it impossible to sleep, I can turn on my Walkman and get six hours of the latest news from foreign capitals, from Paris to Helsinki.

The quality of the radio program has been a continuing topic since the invention of the vacuum tube.

Sixty years ago, when he appeared before a special parliamentary committee on broadcasting, radio pioneer Lee De Forest had this to say: "We look to you in Canada to lead radio in North America out of the morass in which it is pitiably sunk. May Canada fulfill my early dream!"

Did we lead radio out of that morass?

I say yes.

HMCS Alachasse

AT THE OUTBREAK OF WORLD WAR TWO, THE RCMP MADE A GIFT TO the Royal Canadian Navy. It was the redcoats' entire east-coast fleet: the *French*, the *Adversus*, and the *Alachasse*. These were the vessels the redcoats used to thwart the efforts of the rum runners bringing in contraband from the Caribbean.

These were wooden ships, made of layered oak planks for extra weight. The *Alachasse* was 117 feet in length and 14 feet at the beam. If Chief Petty Officer Hart cranked both diesel engines up to the max, it would travel at close to 30 knots, certainly fast enough to catch a sailing vessel with a cargo of what Nellie McClung called "the demon rum."

It was a fluke of timing that made me a member of the *Alachasse* ship's company. One morning in the Signals School I was called to the office and given the news: I was shipping out. I was told to pack and join five other wireless operators —"Sparkers" we were called—who were going to a shore station in Bermuda. We were to leave that afternoon on a destroyer. Believe me, I was one happy *matelot* when I packed my kit bag and said farewell to my buddies in the barracks.

There was just one problem: I had a nagging headache. It was getting worse when I walked through the shipyards, on my way to my rendezvous with my fellow operators. When I was opposite the sick bay I decided that some instant treatment was called for: I nipped in and asked the duty petty officer if he'd give me a couple of aspirins.

"Take off your tunic." This abrupt order startled me. I demurred. I told him I was all packed, and on my way out of the country, and would he please just give me something for a headache. He repeated the order, this time with a little more authority.

Well, well. I was covered with a rosy red rash. Measles. Farewell buddies. Farewell Bermuda. As I put my uniform on again I could hear the petty officer telling personnel to replace me on that draft. I spent 10 miserable days in a temporary hospital with 30 or 40 other victims of this children's disease. Two weeks later I was drafted to the *Alachasse*.

There was a crew of 21; four officers and 17 other ranks. Three of the officers and four of the seamen were from the fishing fleet. We went to sea for a week at a time. When the RCAF spotted an unidentified vessel approaching Canada, they'd give us the co-ordinates and we'd dash off to issue a challenge: we needed information re the vessel and its cargo.

The captain was an Englishman who had been a mate on an Imperial Oil tanker. He was extremely short and extremely round, and I assume it was his shape and weight that one night got us into a pretty pickle.

We were tied up in a busy harbour, and there were two other vessels between the *Alachasse* and the jetty. This means that going ashore, or making the return trip, got rather involved with the gangplanks and railings of other vessels.

On the night in question, I was on duty in the wheelhouse, the only one on board. I spotted the captain approaching and he was, how shall I put this—inebriated. I watched with some fascination as he made his way over the first vessel, and then over the second, but when he got to the *Alachasse* and its gangplank he slipped off and splashed into the drink.

This put me into a spot for which no training was ever provided. I stifled all thoughts of leaving him in there and I did what I felt I had to do: take a boathook, get the end snagged under the collar of his greatcoat, and that was as far as I could go. There was no chance of me hauling him out of the water. It was not at all reassuring to hear that he was in an advanced state of outrage.

At this point, two of my shipmates came aboard. They soon concluded that they couldn't put a lifeboat down where the captain was because he was between *Alachasse* and the neighbouring vessel. There was nothing for me to do but use the boathook to haul the captain around the stern to where the lifeboat was waiting. I felt like an angler with a whale on his lure. It was only when we tried to haul him into the lifeboat did we learn the reason for all the shouts and curses: in his fall he had broken his leg.

We got him into his cabin, and got his clothes off. He wouldn't let us send for help, and only later did I realize the reason why: he wanted to sober up before he got to the sickbay. Believe me, there was a long night of suffering before he would let us send for help.

We were under the command of a substitute captain for 10 or 12 weeks before our old non-friend returned and led us into an even greater disaster. We were just entering the ocean side of the Straits of Canso one evening when the signalman on the bridge noticed that we were headed for a rocky reef. He called down to tell the captain of danger ahead. As was often the case, the captain was in his cups. He told the signalman to mind his own business.

A few minutes later the signalman went down to the wheelhouse and repeated his warning. Again he was told to shut up. Within minutes the *Alachasse* hit the rocks, slid 30 or 40 feet up the reef, and just sat there. When the tide went out we were high and dry.

It was lunch time of the day following when our sister ship arrived to pull us off. What they didn't know—and certainly we didn't—was that the *Alachasse* was impaled. They fastened a six-inch hemp hawser to the bollard on our stern, backed up a bit, and got caught in the current which boils through those straits. When the line tightened it snapped and took off our masts, funnel, and railings. In the course of all of this it took a leg off that signalman and gave three of the rest of us a collection of fractures.

Clearly this called for a court martial, and while the signalman and I were not in attendance, we were represented by the testimony we gave in sworn statements from our hospital beds. The captain was found guilty and stripped—permanently—of command. They gave him a shore job in Port Arthur. When I went there to telegraph, during university vacations, I occasionally saw him on the streets, but with a strategic maneuvre or two always managed to avoid him.

I can't end this without sharing with you a most unusual occurrence. On his vacation in the summer of 1940, our assistant chief engineer was married. He and his bride spent their honeymoon at a country inn on the Nova Scotia Shore. The bride was given to shrieking in orgasmic ecstasy, a fact which alarmed the innkeeper's wife, who called the RCMP.

My shipmate was interviewed regarding the prospect that he was abusing his wife. I've always thought the redcoats had that all wrong; the word should have been "amusing."

Camp Hill Hospital

IT WAS SEPTEMBER 23, 1940, WHEN *HMCS ALACHASSE* HIT THE ROCKS, A date which is engraved on my tiny mind. It was a quartet of army men who got on board (I still don't know how) and tied us down to stretchers and lifted us into lifeboats for the trip to shore. An ambulance was waiting. I can recall that it had the suspension of a stoneboat.

The nearest hospital was St. Martha's, at Antigonish. They made me as comfortable as they could and a doctor told me that the next day I'd be transferred to Halifax for surgery. The following morning one of the nuns came in and asked me if I had "voided." I didn't understand that word used in that manner, but I said no, and went on to say that I hadn't urinated either.

This little exchange led to a tableau that comes to mind every time I visit a hospital. The nun returned, this time carrying a basin covered by a towel. She was not alone. She introduced her company as her newest member of the novitiate. It was the nun's intention to teach her young charge the secrets of that terrible transaction known as "passing the catheter."

What happened next would make a great sequence in a TV drama: it was a brief, absolutely silent test of wills. The novice could not bring herself to touch my penis. While the nun was becoming impatient, the novice at that moment was contemplating another line of work. The silence was broken when the nun said, "Grab hold of it!" It was grabbed and the catheter was inserted and the relief was a blessing.

That afternoon I was transferred to Halifax in the company of my friend Jim Moorman, the signalman who lost his leg. We travelled in another unsprung army ambulance and we became patients in Camp Hill Hospital.

The next morning, after more X-rays and more inspections, a tall friendly doctor introduced himself as Surgeon-

Commander Morton. He pulled a strange piece of hardware out of his breast pocket. "Take a look at this," he said, "You'll never see it again. Tomorrow morning I'm going to use this to fasten together the broken parts of your thigh bone." (He was wrong: I saw it again and I still have it. A year later it was removed in the Winnipeg General.) It was a piece of steel about seven inches in length, with a hole every half-inch. You might have used something like this on the door of the chicken house.

There were 30 of us in Ward M. The largest group was composed of sailors from the Royal Navy, and a small sprinkling of soldiers. (Across the hall was another ward filled with army dispatch drivers who had had accidents with their Norton motor bikes.)

Camp Hill Hospital was a hold-over from the earlier war, and it suffered all the ills of this antiquity. It was so drafty that blankets over windows was a standard winter-time treatment. It was replete with mice, and every night we would feel them running over our blankets; they wanted to get into the snacks some of us kept in our bedside tables. I was backed into a corner in a fracture bed that had a heavy timber structure overhead. From a hole drilled in my shin bone, wires led to a series of weights that hung over the end of the bed. This was low-tech tension.

The nursing sisters were shining jewels, and I can still remember some names: Sister McLean, Sister Kuhn, and another with the improbable name of Sister Brothers. The orderlies were somewhat less praiseworthy. In general they were a cranky lot, perhaps understandable when you think of their work. The service man who got lippy with an orderly faced a true torture test: in the morning he would be given a bedpan that had been left on the outside window ledge all night.

As far as my 29 ward buddies were concerned, I was the perfect model of a "Typhoid Freddie." When my temperature one morning went off the charts, a quick inspection revealed the truth: I had scarlet fever. I was wheeled off to isolation and the whole ward was quarantined: no visitors for the next three weeks. Ward-mates mentioned my name only to curse it.

I was scarcely back in my corner when I complained one day about a sore throat and one more quick diagnosis confirmed still one more problem: diphtheria. By this time I was in a cast that ran from my armpits to my heels. To give me an injection, the doctor first chiseled a hole in the cast over my butt, and then did the painful deed. At this point it was back into solitary, in an isolation hospital on the shores of Bedford basin.

I had private nurses when I was in isolation, and one of them is memorable. The evening shift brought Sister McLean on duty, and one day she arrived looking as if she had been in a car accident; her face was beet red and her eyes were nearly swollen shut.

I quickly diagnosed her case as an advanced case of infatuation. Her beloved was a member of the RCMP, who served in her home village down the shore. It was his practice to come to Halifax for the weekends so they could be together. Only this morning, she sobbed, she had learned that he was in Halifax last weekend, "and he didn't even (boo-hoo) call me."

As I soon determined, I had no option but to engage in some role reversal: I would play the role of Fred the love counsellor; I would be the nurse and she would become the patient. All that evening, backed by nothing more than the wisdom of my full 19 years, I elaborated on what my aunt in Winnipeg often told her daughters: "Boyfriends are like street cars; if you miss one, there'll be another one along in 7 1/2 minutes."

More Camp Hill memories. We were a giant institution in mourning at Christmas time, 1940, when a favourite intern lost his life in an auto accident. We had a popular topic; our most unusual visitor was a tall naval captain who—believe it or not—carried a long, brass-bound telescope (known as his peepstick) under his arm. This was the Irish-born Captain Fogarty Fagan, who commanded an armed merchantman.

One night, early in the spring of '41, the lights went on in our ward at 3 a.m., and a battalion of workers began moving out the patients. I was the only one left; my fracture bed wouldn't go through the doors. Within minutes the replacement patients arrived, some of them on foot, some in wheelchairs, some on stretchers. These were the only survivors of the *Jervis Bey,* that armed merchantman captained by Fogarty Fagan. One of them became my close friend in the next couple of months. He was Samuel Patience, a giant Scot, on whose behalf radio station CHNS put out a request for some slippers, size 15.

Within a few days this story filled the media; when Captain Fagan saw that the battleship *Bismarck* was about to attack the convoy he was protecting, he charged the *Bismarck* with all guns blazing. By the time the *Jervis Bey* was blown out of the water, the ships in the convoy had dispersed, and the *Bismarck* never caught up with one of them. Fagan lost his life but posthumously was awarded the Victoria Cross.

There came a day, and glorious it was, when I was to be cut out of my cast. The doctor, who was proud of the new set of shears, asked me if it contained any metal. I said no. Crunch! He struck metal and he said a rude word. I forgot to tell him that inside the cast were several long nail files the nurses had given me so I could scratch.

Freed of my plaster cocoon for the first time in nine months, I was asked what I wanted first. I said I wanted a bath. I was just being lowered into the rub when the air-raid siren blasted off and they hurried me back to the ward. More rude words.

The Jesuits

"McGuinness, I just checked the record. You've been here for two weeks and you still haven't stated what your sports connection will be."

The speaker was Father Sutton, rector of St. Paul's College, Winnipeg, in 1941. When he challenged me with that statement, I looked at him in disbelief. After all, I had lost 40 pounds in most of a year in hospital, I had a brace on one leg, I had to use a cane, and this man wanted me to get into sports. Did he think I could be quarterback of the Crusaders?

When I suggested that perhaps it would be a while before I was an active participant in the jock world, he said "Rubbish! There is something you can do, walking stick or not. Go and see the coaches. Let me hear from you by the end of the week."

I limped out of his office and down the hall, feeling dreadfully put-upon. I knew there was an answer to the problem, I just didn't know what it might be. I was certain of only one thing: I was living in the only institution that was willing to put me on an accelerated trip through high school.

Joy! I found an answer to my conundrum after a few minutes with the senior hockey coach. Later that day I told Father Sutton that I now was manger of the senior hockey team. I still wasn't highly mobile, but I could certainly operate a telephone and buy sticks, book buses and schedule games.

It may sound like a paradox, but I am a Protestant who is a cheerleader for the Society of Jesus. For three years I lived in a residence with a number of Jesuits, and student Jesuits, so I can claim to have had a close acquaintance with these unusual men.

This story begins in the autumn of 1941. I was home from the navy, but I wasn't in great shape. I was mobile but only with difficulty: I had a heavy metal caliper splint on my left leg and I needed a walking stick. I was 20 by this time; I had to go back to grade nine, and the question was: where should I attend school?

I took my problem to my guide, mentor and uncle, Dr. Fred McGuinness, an obstetrician in Winnipeg. He called a friend in the Department of Education. After listening to my history, the educator had an idea: he said if I belonged to him, he'd put me in St. Paul's. There were major advantages: I could live in the same building in which I studied, and one things more: the department would set special exams for me any time the Jesuits said I was ready to write them.

Father Sutton had a commendable attitude toward the non-Catholics; at the beginning of each term he convened us in the Common Room and gave us a brief lecture: he and the other priests would appreciate silence on our part when the Roman Catholics were in chapel. It was easy for us to meet this condition.

We had students in every grade from one to fourth-year university. The university curriculum was not complete, however, which meant that for some classes our students attended United College of the University of Manitoba.

Many of the boarders were from remote settlements: hydro-generating stations, northern construction sites, fur-trade outposts, and they had only two options for education. They could leave home and become boarders, or they could take their training at home via correspondence. I often wished some of those lonely little punks in the first three grades had stayed at home.

The heart of the institution was the refectory. It consisted of two rooms: a large one for the boarders, and a small private one for the priests. By tradition they ate in silence while one of the younger ones read from current literature.

I'd like to say that the cuisine rated as five-star Michelin quality, but I'd be lying. The cooking was done by a group of nuns who may have been imported from Europe for English obviously was their second language. No one starved to death of which I am aware, for there was always plenty of bread, potatoes, and a generic type of gravy.

Someone in that kitchen was fascinated by chocolate pudding, a regular item for our dessert. As a silent protest, a student one day flipped a spoonful of this gelatinous concoction at the wall. It hit with a splat, and slowly worked its way down to floor level. This led to heavy action on the part of Father McDonald, the disciplinarian. We were lectured that we must at all times be aware that in our numbers there was an agent of the devil. That mess stayed on the wall all year.

Sports was a dominant factor at St. Paul's, and every Friday evening in the autumn we proved this. We could walk from the college grounds to the old Osborne Stadium for the games of the Winnipeg high school football league. Young students, old students, young priests, old priests, the school spirit demanded our attendance. A standard joke on the campus in those years was the injunction leveled at an earlier team by coach Greg Kabat, at that time a standout on the Winnipeg Blue Bombers. "Remember that you're from St. Paul's. Remember that you're Crusaders. Be gentlemen and be sportsmen—once you're three touchdowns ahead."

St. Paul's had a bursar named Father Kelly, who was notoriously close with a nickel. It was his standing practice to put a nickel on the bill of every boarder if anyone dropped a dish in the refectory. When student Albert McCruden did some elementary mathematics he concluded that every smashed dish yielded $15 to the bursar, which meant, as we were informed, "This place doesn't run on the gold standard, but rather on the crockery standard."

For the boarders, the regimen was a killer. In the morning there was a one-hour study session before classes began, and a two-hour session every evening. Only between four and six each afternoon was there any free time. It may have been heavy-duty scholastics, but it worked. As proof I can recite the list of MPs, senators, judges, doctors, lawyers, and engineers from among my classmates. One with whom I keep in touch is Gildas Molgat, Speaker of the Senate.

A knock on the door one evening interrupted my studies. At the door was Father St. Jacques, who doubled in brass as a history teacher at the same time he was an RCAF chaplain with the rank of squadron leader. He was a non-Jesuit, as you are about to learn.

"McGuinness," he said, "You are the only student who is old enough to have a liquor permit. Right?" I concurred. He then asked me if there was sufficient room on my permit for a bottle of whiskey. I said yes. He then asked me to get into his car so he could drive me to the liquor store.

I put up a mild protest. I said I couldn't possibly spare the time. After all, I had a history examination the next morning, as he knew, being the teacher.

"Get in the car," he said, "And stop worrying about that exam. You're going to get a B+." I did as I was bid, and ever since have wondered why I didn't hold out for an A.

One class that I really enjoyed was the Friday afternoon session in elocution. The Jesuits treated this as a serious subject, for which the students had to be prepared. Anyone who wants to hear my rendering of "The White Cliffs of Dover," by Alice Duer Miller, need only ask.

Winnipeg

Dots And Dashes

IF THIS BOOK HAD SOUND, I WOULD BEGIN THIS LETTER WITH THE CHATTER of a telegraph sounder.

You probably didn't know it, but I am thoroughly bilingual. I can communicate—up to a point—in English. I can also communicate in the Morse code, or rather I should be more specific, in the Morse codes—plural.

When I was a telegrapher (note that emphasis) for Canadian Pacific Telegraphs, I used what is called the landline code, which consists of dots, dashes, and spaces.

In the navy, where they called me a telegraphist, I used the radio code, dots and dashes only. There are half a dozen different letters between those two codes, plus most of the numbers and articles of punctuation.

As a telegrapher, I worked exclusively in the commercial end of things. The office was on the second floor right on the corner of Portage and Main, in Winnipeg. Almost all of our business was cables, telegrams, press dispatches.

My special interest was in those dispatches. Because I had little seniority, I was almost always on the least popular shift—from 5:30 in the afternoon to one o'clock in the morning. This was also the period in which most of the press copy was moved.

Because I came back from overseas service early, I was telegraphing during the last three years of the war. A lot of those press dispatches I copied every evening had to do with the battles in Europe.

Every evening for over a year I copied the European dispatches written by Ross Munro. In later years, when the two of us were publishers of Southam newspapers, we often talked about this experience, especially about the code he and the other war correspondents used in order to keep the word count to a minimum.

This code was not at all involved, but it did make for some tricky copying. They simply omitted all articles and indefinite articles and conjunctions; the copy read like a thousand-word-long headline.

One other regular assignment was enough to turn me into a pacifist: For six evenings a week, apart from a 20-minute break, I copied casualty telegrams from Ottawa. Twenty or thirty times each hour I typed another telegram which began, "The minister of national defense regrets to inform you that your son is..." and then came the bad news. The subject of this telegram was either: wounded, killed in action, missing in action, or a prisoner of war.

I had occasional breaks from the office, and they were always interesting.

In those days there were no teletypes, so there were telegraph operators in the newsrooms of the major newspapers. I supplied the vacation relief one summer for an operator named Tingley at the *Winnipeg Free Press*; and later for a man named Bill Baizley, at the *Winnipeg Tribune*.

Oh yes, Bill Baizley. This was a man with an extraordinary typing talent. Friend Bill had only one arm, but he could type at the same speed as the rest of us.

At the same time we had another one-armed telegrapher, Dave Kell. It always made a good office story on that day in the late autumn when these two men set off on their lunch hour for a trip to Eaton's; they wanted to buy their winter gloves: one needed the right one; the other the left.

I have a sharp flashback every time I hear of someone losing his job to technology.

Heavens, this happened to me when I was only 23. As I worked with my dots and dashes and spaces, there was a machine at the end of the office that was hooked up on an experimental basis. It was called the Morkham-Kleinschmidt printer, which was abbreviated to "mux," which later became teletype. This turned into the mechanical monster which eventually spelled the end of (sniff) the Morse era.

And that's the end of this story.

Royal American Shows

It all began when I was asked to return a telephone call to Des Moines, Iowa. I did as I was bid and five minutes later was on the payroll of Royal American.

The man who took that call was Harry Julius, an executive with the biggest carnival in the world. We had met the year before when he was on the Class A. exhibition circuit on the Prairies with Royal American, and I was along as good shepherd to some federal displays.

The reason for the call? When Royal American arrived in Des Moines, one of the first ports of call on their six-month work year, their publicity man had fallen ill and was now in hospital. It appeared that the carnival had to face the western circuit minus what they called their" director of publicity and exploitation." Could I lend a hand?

I could and I did. My display duties kept me busy every day from ten to six; I could work for Royal American four hours every evening. I did their promotional writing; I was host to any members of the media who visited the midway. Once a week I wrote a lengthy report on midway activities and sent it by wire to *Billboard*, the Bible of outdoor show business.

For those *Billboard* stories I interviewed some interesting characters. The concessions manager was Sam Gordon, who was happy to be quoted on his introduction to show business. For years this has been my model of underhandedness. At the 1938 World's Fair in Chicago he was a ticket seller, a job for which he paid, repeat paid, $60 per week. He made that back, and a lot more besides, by short-changing the patrons.

Another interesting interview was a group of students from the U. of Oklahoma who signed up to be the chorus line in the Moulin Rouge. The job was a perfect fit for their vacation period. One of them had her master's degree on the life of Chaucer.

Now, it will not surprise you to hear that the carnival was mobile; but you might like to know just how good this show was in the footloose department.

Six hours after arriving on a bare piece of pasture, with no hydro, no sewer, no water, Joe Pontico's cookhouse would be in business. Four hours later between 45 and 50 riding devices would be active; two hours later the midway would be operating. There was enough hydro power for a small city. Royal American bought six giant generators from the U.S. government. They were the type built for service personnel setting up shop on uninhabited islands in the South Pacific.

The big money, and the basis for most publicity was "The Moulin Rouge," a vaudeville show which always featured a newsworthy headliner: Sally Rand, Gypsy Rose Lee, and Bonnie Baker were some of them.

In the same vein of straight entertainment was "Harlem in Havana" with an all-black crew and cast. Leon Claxton, the producer-director, had a recruitment practice I thought unique. When the tour began, every member of his band was equipped with a brand-new instrument, the best that Boosie and Hawkes could provide. If they went the distance, it was theirs.

The man who assembled this show was a dynamic organizer; Carl J. Sedlmayr. He was not only the owner, but he was in charge of every aspect. He knew so much about midway goings-on that some of his employees thought he was a modern Janus, with eyes in the back of his head. By the end of the second year, I knew his secret. On a regular basis he would ask the operator of the Ferris Wheel to give him a ride to the top, and to leave him there. From this aerie he developed a list of those who were goofing-off.

This was an elemental society. If you had power, you used it. Every employee knew that if he failed to shape up, all his supervisor had to do was call the immigration department and ask that the employee be expelled. They'd be delivered to the nearest border-crossing point.

Money was both king and queen. If you failed to tip the lay-out man—handsomely—your location might be on the other side of the barns. If you failed to tip the mailman—handsomely—no mail for you. If you failed to tip the loading crew—handsomely—you'd be the last, very last, to get your stuff on the train.

What put Royal American into deep disgrace, and made it a virtual fugitive from Canadian justice, was a series of events so bizarre that it's still hard to believe they're true.

Twice in the mid '70s, once in Saskatoon and once in Edmonton, passengers boarding flights to Vancouver in fair week asked if they could have preferential service: they wanted their luggage inspected in the offices of the RCMP. In both cases, these suitcases were filled with money, tens of thousands of dollars' worth. When this word got to the intelligence branch they leaped to an erroneous conclusion that this was a drug operation. This led to a dawn raid on Royal American with city police, RCMP, tax auditors and related snoops.

They found no evidence of a drug operation, but they did uncover larcenous practices that had been carried on for years. Royal American had been bribing exhibition officials with expensive gifts, and in come cases hard cash, in return for contracts to be the carnival operator for the Class A. circuit. The Government of Alberta, where the raid took place, established a one-judge board of enquiry and his report sets out chapter and verse of a sorry story. End of Royal American in Canada.

What I saw every summer for five in a row was proof of that curious marriage of convenience which brings together a carnival and an agricultural fair. On their own, neither will keep those turnstiles turning. Put them together and you may just have a winning combo.

Early CBC

I HAVE A PROFOUND BELIEF IN SERENDIPITY. THIS IS THE NEAR-SCIENCE of making the joyful discovery. You make a serendipitous discovery when you are searching for one thing and you find something else of value.

This happened to me one day. I was involved with a series of dispatch boxes in the basement, searching for a file I have not opened in years. In the course of this search I found a copy of the first manuscript I ever sold to CBC.

The year was 1947. The location was Winnipeg. The CBC in those days was located on a floor in the Manitoba Telephone Building on Portage Avenue East.

The director of programming at that time was Kathleen MacIver. She bought a story I wrote after a tour of what was then called the "Class A. Circuit." This circuit involved five major agricultural exhibitions: Brandon, Calgary, Edmonton, Saskatoon, and Regina. There were several thousand of us who visited all these shows.

This was quite a crew: jockeys and race horses; federal technicians who tested the urine of those horses; tax men who collected the federal share of the purse; agricultural scientists who put on demonstrations; operators of commercial displays; and I mustn't overlook the carnival, Royal American Shows with its 1,000 employees.

Anyway, that was my story, and in those days every commentary was 14 minutes in length. The recording was done on a purple disk, the size of a dinner plate. If I were to cough, or sneeze, or really mess up my lines, well, Kay McIver would give me the high-sign from the control room and I would start over again.

All of this serves to remind me of some of the early CBC characters I met and worked with, or interviewed.

In the Winnipeg newsroom in those days one cheery fixture was Peter B. Whittall, a farm commentator. Pete went on to become one of the early television regulars as Mr. Fix-It.

Peter also went on to raise a storm of controversy with one of those quips he tossed off so easily. It happened on one of his noon-time farm broadcasts. That morning he had driven Mrs. Whittall to the hospital where she was about to deliver a child. While Peter was on the air, a producer tip-toed into the studio and laid a note on his desk. It read: "It's a girl, 5 1/2 pounds."

Peter interrupted his broadcast just long enough to read this aloud, following which he said, "Good heavens: I hardly got my seed back." Those of us who thought this was a clever farm-boy come-back were far, far outnumbered by early feminists who felt he had besmirched motherhood.

For a year, in my student days in Winnipeg, I had lived in the home of an aunt. It was located right behind Fort Osborne Barracks. One summer day I was trimming Auntie's hedge, and a young soldier stopped for a chat.

This was Wally Koster, at that time a member of the regimental band. We became friends. I always viewed him as having an unusual blend of talents: on Saturday night I could go to the Winnipeg Auditorium and listen to him as he sang with the dance band.

On Sunday night I could go the old Olympic Rink on North Main Street and watch as he played semi-professional hockey. In later years I had four trips per year to Toronto on newspaper business, and Wally and I would often have lunch in the old Celebrity Club.

When I was at the *Medicine Hat News* I was always on the search for a subject of a weekly column. I had a special interest in persons who had once lived in "The Hat."

When I read that Bruno Gerussi had been born in Medicine Hat I made arrangements to interview him on my next trip to Toronto. Let us agree that Bruno's connection with the Gas City was a slight one.

His parents arrived in Canada from Italy, en route to the coal mines in the Crowsnest Pass. As the train was nearing Medicine Hat, Mrs. Gerussi went into labour. Bruno indeed was delivered in the Medicine Hat Hospital, but a couple of days later he and his mother left, never to return.

In my reading of the old files of the *Medicine Hat News* I often noted something peculiar; in the early days one reporter always signed his stories with his initials, RCG.

Upon enquiry, I learned that this was the grand-daddy of the CBC performers, R. Clyde Gilmour.

Why did he always put his initials on his stories? Rumour has it that the editor of the moment was rather uncertain about young Clyde's reportorial skills, so he made him sign his stories to separate them from the rest of the crew in the newsroom.

One last big name from yesteryear. As everyone interested in the history of Medicine Hat knows, the first store to open was that of Tweed and Ewart. Or it may have been Ewart and Tweed, I forget.

Anyway, that Tweed was an early descendant of the man who called himself T. Tweed, the irrepressible Tommy. We invited him back home once for an historical occasion, and it fell my honour to pick him up at the Calgary airport and deliver him to "The Hat." Let me assure you that not only was this man a great character actor; he was also a great character.

At a time like this it's tempting to say that they don't make characters like these any more—but I know I'd be wrong. I'm certain that Mother Corporation has replacement characters in all categories... it's just that I haven't met them.

Saskatchewan

Hollywood Comes To Maple Creek

BECAUSE I AM A COUNTRY-DWELLER, I USE A SATELLITE DISH FOR TV watching. It may surprise you to learn that while we have close to 300 channels from which to choose, some evenings we do what we should have done in the first place—turn the dratted thing off and open our current reading material.

But I mustn't digress. I find that some old movies beget long-lost memories.

I was flicking through the channels and I came across an old horse opera starring Alan Ladd. I had an immediate flashback to the early '50s when Mr. Ladd inadvertently got me involved in an unusual project.

At the time a large number of us were preparing for Saskatchewan's birthday party in 1955.

One of the members of our board of directors read in an entertainment column that Hollywood was about to make a movie called "Saskatchewan." It would star Alan Ladd.

Well, this became an item on the agenda of our next meeting and I was instructed to "do something about it." After all, it might be a publicity coup if we could have a movie named "Saskatchewan" produced in the province with the same name.

I called Universal-International Studios, in Hollywood. The operator listened to my story and put me right through to the department she called "Exploitation." This was my introduction to the names of individuals in and around show business: my call was taken by Jack O. Diamonds.

Jack (we soon were on a first-name basis) listened to my story and said he would call me back. Inside an hour, he did so and the news was encouraging. If I were to go to Hollywood, the producer and director of *Saskatchewan* would give me a hearing.

And they did. For part of one morning they pored over pictures I showed them of Saskatchewan's wide, open spaces, and agreed to see me later that afternoon. My new friend, Jack O. Diamonds, took me to the commissary where we had lunch with Charlton Heston, who was at work that day on another western.

The upshot of all of this was that Universal-International wanted to see me in Calgary in a couple of weeks' time, as they were also scouting out that province as a possible site. At our meeting in Calgary I was to give them more assurance that we had vast acreages without any of the trappings of society, i.e. hydro poles; and that in that area there were ranchers with hundreds of horses they would lease.

My trip from Regina to Calgary was historic in itself. I travelled with my friend and fellow committee member, Dr. John Archer, a noted historian. There was no black-topped Trans-Canada Highway in those days and we made our trip in a driving rain without missing a mudhole. At Calgary the meeting went well. The movie folk promised to meet us in a week's time in that place which calls itself "The Old Cowtown," also known as Maple Creek.

I can recall every part of this event. John Archer and I lived alongside the movie-makers in the Commercial Hotel. We dined in the Star Cafe. We drove around a territory so vast and open that it is almost scary.

The second morning, by arrangement, the men from Universal-International met the district ranchers. They soon agreed on the terms and conditions regarding a large herd of horses. Really, at this point, friend John and I felt we had the movie practically in hand.

And then IT happened; the rains came back. A deluge. The next morning the Hollywooders decided they wanted another look at those vast open spaces. We drove them south of town, and when we left the highway to turn around, we became hopelessly stuck in the mud.

From the back seat John and I could hear mutterings about how heavy equipment like their sound trucks and trailers could never navigate through mud like this—and right at that point our dreams of glory fell apart.

The movie named "Saskatchewan" was made in Alberta. Alan Ladd indeed was the star. This epic stank up movie houses clear across the continent. The reviews were so bad that the residents of the real Saskatchewan lamented having the provincial name on a thing that awful.

Thus endeth my total experience with Hollywood. Interesting... flashy.... artificial.... but also memorable.

A Tiny Investment That Changed My Life

THIS IS THE STORY OF AN INVESTMENT. THE SURPRISING THING ABOUT it is, it was only fifty cents, but it changed my life. It turned me into a social historian, of the amateur type.

This all took place in the early '50s. I went to the Land Titles office in Regina. I placed two quarters on the counter and asked the clerk if he would show me the documentation on Section .22. 15: 02, west of the second.

In a few minutes he came back, carrying a large heavy volume. He opened it at the appropriate page and at the bottom I saw something I had never seen before: the signatures of my grandparents. This document was the title of their homestead quarter.

Well, this was a moving experience. It caused me to think that I had known persons who made history. After all, they were among that flood of settlers who filled up Canada's Bread Basket, the Great Plains between the Red and the Rockies.

This was my introduction to local history, and social history. These subjects quickly replaced that other type of history which I had disliked so heartily in school: The Wars of the Roses, the Pelopennisian War, the names of the crowned heads of Europe.

I made enquiries about my grandparents and learned enough of their story to write about it for *Reader's Digest.* I became a collector of local history books. As I did so I learned a great deal more about those persons from many lands who gave Canada her unique characteristics.

As I read those books of local history I did so with a notebook beside me: I like to keep track of stories in two categories—the oddities, and those I call inspirational.

Oddities first.

In the history of Springfield, the first rural municipality in Manitoba, I read about the Laird Brothers. In 1931, when they needed food for their fox farm, they contracted with farmers of North Dakota for boxcar loads of frozen jackrabbits. There are photographs of these boxcars being unloaded of a commodity never considered by NAFTA.

When Sandy Waddell was working on his farm near the Roseau River, he saw what he thought was a monster in the shallows. He had an axe with him so he slew the monster: it was a giant fresh-water sturgeon. Exact length—brace yourselves—15 feet, six inches—weight 400 pounds. He needed a team to get it home.

This story is from the history of Dominion City. In case you think it's a fish story, think again. This whopper was hoisted up to the branch of a tree so this moment in history could be suitably recorded in photographs.

I have collected stories of what might be Divine Intervention.

In the book, *West of the Turtle Mountains*, there's a story from 1929. Farmer John Nestibo, of Goodlands, was visited by his neighbour, Grandmaö Korbell. She dreamt that the Lord had given her a message, and she was to deliver it to John Nestibo as quickly as she could. The message was that he should sell his grain immediately.

Well, he tried to but he didn't. Nestibo went to the grain elevator and attempted to sell his inventory, valued at $20,000, but he was talked out of it by the elevator operator who assured him that the price of grain was certain to go up. Shortly afterward the market collapsed.

In another book, *Beyond Beginnings*, written by a committee of volunteers at Eriksdale, Manitoba, I read about Lorna Anderson. I later interviewed this remarkable woman who twice has recovered from life-threatening experiences with cancer. The last one involved the removal of a 16-pound tumor from her uterus.

In the period of her recovery, Lorna Anderson dreamt that she had a conversation with God. A deal was struck. In return for saving her life, she would raise money for other cancer victims. She did so in a highly publicized walk from Thunder Bay to Eriksdale in which she raised $53,000 for cancer research.

When I suggested to Mrs. Anderson, a retired postal worker, that perhaps she had kept her end of the bargain, she disagreed. She's hard at work planning a second stroll down the Trans-Canada Highway, this time from Banff to Eriksdale. I'll wager that she makes it.

If you care to be inspired about the human spirit at work, let me tell you about "One-Eyed" Johnson, a trapper who lived near Ignace, Ontario. Johnson lived alone, a long way from a neighbour. When he broke his leg, he knew what had to be done: he needed traction. He devised a block-and-tackle, set the bone himself, and managed to survive during the recovery.

Over the years, in many different ways, I have used the story of Chris Vestre, of Strongfield, Saskatchewan. Chris and his wife were settlers from Finland. They could not speak English. They desperately wanted to settle on one particular quarter-section because it was surrounded by Finnish-speaking neighbours.

Now, there was a reason why that quarter-section was vacant: no one had ever been able to locate a source of water. But the Vestres were not daunted. They went to work.

Listen carefully now: with Chris and a shovel, and Mrs. Vestre hauling the dirt and stones to the surface with a pail, they dug 17 dry wells. Fortunately for them, they had pioneer perseverance; on their 18th try they struck a source of pure, clear water. They did well as farmers, and I know this because over the years I have chatted with their descendants.

Canada has 20,000 local-history books, and I wish we had that many again. They generally are written in response to a significant anniversary: a jubilee or a centennial.

Well, here we are on the eve of the millennium, and I hope our volunteer scribes get busy. Individuals who work on local-history books always end up with a new appreciation not only of their home communities, but also of the nation itself.

Life In The Wheat Province

"I'LL BE OVER IN AN HOUR. I JUST SAT DOWN TO EAT." WHEN MY brother-in-law hung up the telephone he turned to me and told me I was going to be busy that evening.

The speaker was Dr. Robert Inglis, at that time (I think) the only practitioner in Estevan. As he explained it, the local abortionist had had a fall and had dislocated his shoulder. He would have to be treated at home because the nuns at St. Joseph's Hospital had banned him from entering their premises—ever. (He was a former doctor who had lost his license.)

During all this discourse, Bob never ever mentioned what my responsibilities were to be, but this became clear once we got into the patient's living room: I was to be the anesthetist.

The patient was prone on his living room floor. First, Bob Inglis took off his right shoe, and then began to administer the chloroform. When he had the patient safely under, he then directed me to sit down by the patient's head and maintain a steady drip into the cone. At that point Bob put his foot in the patient's armpit, grasped the patient's hand, and began the manipulations which set things right.

I can be precise about the date I practiced medicine: 16 March, 1953. I know this because the next day was St. Patrick's, and here again there was a memorable event. My sister Dorreene asked me not to drive to Regina on St. Pat's Day; there was a blizzard warning. But, I had promised to be home that day and away I went.

I was just passing Yellowgrass when I came across a bunch of cars and trucks blocking the highway. A load of hogs had been blown off the road and volunteers were attempting to get it back on. Urging them on and acting like the supervisor was a short man in mangy old 'coon coat and hat. He looked familiar but I couldn't put a name on him.

When I got out of my car, this busy one came over and asked me if I was the fellow who was working on the Saskatchewan history project. I said yes. He then told me that I should record the fact that on St. Patrick's Day, 1953, I saw Father Athol Murray pushing a load of pigs to market. What's more, he said, they were Jewish pigs, the property of Sam Pechet of Yellowgrass, who owned the Nelson Hotel at Carberry.

I had so many memorable days in Saskatchewan that I sometimes think I could fill a five-foot shelf with memories. Like the day I saw a car hit a tree.

I was on my way to work one morning, driving east on Victoria Avenue in Regina, when the car ahead of me went out of control, mounted the median, and struck a tree. I parked and ran to help. I opened the door and saw that the driver was the most popular man Saskatchewan ever produced, His Honor, Lieutenant-Governor "Billy" Patterson. He was unconscious, but I didn't know if it was from the accident, or the liquor to which he was addicted. He had a bad cut over his left eye, but I knew he was breathing.

Because I didn't want passersby to see him in this condition, I pushed him over to the passenger's side and proceeded to drive his car away. When I was coming down off the median, I had to apply the brakes, which I did with some vigour. I had never used power brakes before and the results were dramatic; not only did we stop in a hurry, but my passenger was propelled forward and his head hit the dashboard with a terrible thump. This time he got a cut over the right eye.

After I had delivered him to the emergency ward of the hospital, I went to the Hotel Saskatchewan, where he lived, and gave the keys to the desk clerk. He was not surprised to hear what had happened. A couple of weeks later His Honor called on me in my office and thanked me for my help.

Billy Patterson literally gave his life to Saskatchewan, as long-time MLA, then premier, then lieutenant-governor. It was a tragedy that he ended up stoney broke. I have always admired what T.C. Douglas did when he learned of this: he called in the president of the Liberal Party and offered him a deal: if the Liberals would buy Mr. and Mrs. Patterson a house, the NDP government would give them a pension for life. On a handshake this notable arrangement was confirmed.

From an official point of view, my employer in Saskatchewan was Mr. Justice Edward Culliton, of the Court of Appeal. Judge Culliton was chairman of the Saskatchewan Golden Jubilee Committee, of which I was the executive director. But Premier Douglas liked to be kept abreast of how our jubilee plans were developing, and this led me into a score or more of interesting trips. If "T.C." knew that he had a same-day trip to one of the towns, he'd often call and ask me to drive him so we could chat about the birthday-party plans.

(We had a curious connection, T.C. Douglas and me. We both had active cases of the bone disease osteomyelitis. Mine drained constantly from a sinus in my left thigh; five days a week I visited a public-health clinic to get the dressings changed. In the premier's case, his drained only occasionally. Several times he called me in the middle of the night to ask if I had any golden bullets in the refrigerator. This meant that his temperature was rising and a flare-up was imminent. We lived only a block apart so a delivery was easy. Those bullets of which he spoke were pills of tetracycline which helped keep my "osteo" under control. DVA kept me supplied with this drug. I kept "T.C." supplied.)

As I came to know the premier better, I learned a great deal about his unusual characteristics. One of them required that he must always be prepared if he was going to speak in public. On the night on which Douglas spoke on national TV, after having just lost an important election, he smiled into the camera and said, "Now, I'll lay me down and bleed a while and then get up and fight again."

This is typically Douglas, I said to myself. I believed there were thousands of Canadians watching the TV screen who marveled at this man's ability to toss off a quote that was precisely right for the moment. What they couldn't know, if they didn't know him, is that few of his comments were casual. I say he went to the event that evening with notes for two mini-speeches in his pocket, one for each possibility.

In preparation for one of our out-of-town trips, I was parked one morning in front of the Legislative Buildings, waiting for him. We were supposed to leave for the official opening of a new school a couple of hours' driving time away. When the premier showed up, an hour late, he was steaming with anger.

He asked me if I could handle a riddle. I said I'd try. "What's the difference between a cactus and a caucus?" he asked. I confessed that I had no idea. The answer is, with a cactus the pricks are on the outside. In the Regina paper a couple of days later I learned that the CCF caucus had voted down one of his favourite projects.

While Douglas was a master of the quip, this was only on a calculated basis. Several times he told me how he lamented the millions of jokes that are wasted because they are told out of context. He had a sterling example of the right joke in the right setting.

"Imagine," he explained, "that you and I leave the Legislative Building and we head into town. We come to an intersection and we have the green light but an extremely pregnant lady steps off the curb right in front of us. At this point, the quipster who is on top of his work, rolls down his window, leans out, and says, 'You should be more careful Madam; you can get knocked down, too.'"

Medicine Hat

Oddities From The Hat

ISN'T IT ODD, THAT SO MANY OF MY HAPPIEST MEMORIES OF LIFE in The Hat concern a collection of oddities.

In an earlier period if you had showed up at the counter of the *Medicine Hat News* with a classified ad, and if the staff was in a benevolent mood, and they usually were if you had cash in your hand, they'd put your tiny bulletin on page one under the heading, "Too Late To Classify." And that's what you're going to get right now, oddities too late to classify.

To me Medicine Hat means Harry Veiner, he of the big hat, he of the big Buick cars which always showed a lot of wear.

Oh, I may be shaky on the numbers, but I have a recollection that the first time he stood for Parliament, he suffered a heavy loss, perhaps by thousands of votes. On try #2 he made an improvement; I believe he lost that time by only 600. If you extrapolate these numbers, it appeared to most of us that Harry was a shoo-in when he tried a third time. He wasn't.

In the aftermath I had lunch with him one day at the Cypress Club and I asked him why he kept on running for the MP's job. He thought for only a minute before he gave me a great example of folk wisdom.

"Playing in politics reminds me of the woman who stands at the door of the maternity hospital with a new baby in her arms. She says, "Well, that was a great experience... but I'm never going to repeat it!" And guess what? A year later she's coming down those same steps with still another bundle in her arms."

I could only conclude that Harry lost those elections for the federal seat because the voters wanted to keep him at home. Certainly he was a consummate politician. He knew what his electorate wanted; a low mill rate, recreation facilities, and black-topped streets.

When I think of The Hat, strange stories come to mind. One morning Sgt. Ernie Kumm of the RCMP telephoned. Big Ernie boomed into my ear the news that he had an urgent message for the driver of a California car with license TB 365. Would I put it in the paper?

I said no, that would not be necessary. To find that car all he had to do was go to unit #21 of the Horseshoe Motel at Swift Current. Ernie was dumbfounded. Then I explained. I'd stayed there the night before, and this car was parked alongside mine. Why did I remember the plate number? Because it occurred to me that it was an anagram for tuberculosis, every day of the year.

Ernie was transferred to Red Deer, which gets me into another Kumm story. On our way back from a Lions' convention in Edmonton, where I'd been the luncheon speaker, Lion John Weimer asked me if I'd drive his car for a while. I did. I drove it right into an RCMP speed trap, and my former friend, Lion Ernie Kumm gave me a ticket. Next week in police court, Lion A.Y. Spivack, the magistrate, relieved me of $34. A pox on Lions, I say.

When you're in the news business you soon learn that you can never foretell which stories may ring the bell with the journalists. For proof, let me tell you of a story in The News in the early '60s.

It was only a couple of paragraphs long, but it traveled all over North America; it told of the Redcliff fire chief being disciplined for using the oxygen in his emergency tanks. When he came to work with a hangover, a few whiffs of the stuff would make a new man out of him.

Well, the calls requesting confirmation came in from all over the continent, from Halifax on one side to Los Angeles on the other. We even had the dubious distinction of being quoted in *Time*, a publication my loathing for which increases by squares. Three times when I was in The Hat, *Time* interviewed me. Three times they changed my quotes to fit their slant. A pox on that magazine.

For a happy memory, let me tell you about bonspiel week. Most lunch hours during this annual event I would go to a room on the second floor of the Assiniboia Hotel and visit with the drawmaster, friend Pudge McCallum. I'd take with me lunch for two, and we'd chat while he maintained his wall charts which recorded who was to play where and when.

During one bonspiel I chatted on the street corner with Henry Mitchell, who snorted with derision as he saw curlers pass by in their tams and sweaters, swinging their brooms. To Henry, "This is a hell of a lot of trouble to go to, just to get drunk."

Back at the office I put these words in the mouth of my alter ego, Medicine Hattie. Some of Hattie's comments were taken humorously, but not this one.

Strangest memory of all? Here it comes. I was working late at the office one night, and when I left I pulled in behind another car crossing Finlay Bridge. Halfway across the car ahead of me stopped. The driver got out, climbed to the top of the railing, and jumped.

I ran to the office, called the police, and they arrived just as the leaper waded ashore on the north side. It seems he hit a shallow spot, which helped him decide the world wasn't such a cruel place after all.

Shortgrass Country

TO GET A FEELING FOR THE SHORTGRASS COUNTRY YOU NEED TO DO more than visit Medicine Hat; you've got to tour the territory.

Mind you, to do so calls for a heap of mileage. If you want to examine that area bounded by Maple Creek, Manyberries, Foremost, Bindloss, Brooks, and Empress, you'll drive through country which to the uninitiated appears unused, unloved, and uninhabited. It's none of those things, but these may be your first impressions.

My first forays were in response to invitations from ranchers, and scientists working in the beef business. I still have in my library a set of booklets which tell of the research conducted at Manyberries Range Station by Hobart Peters. It took years to prove that a beef-buffalo cross is not going to work, although if you read the farm papers this get-rich-quick prospect still comes around once a decade.

Besides those booklets I have memories of the ranches. I soon learned my way to the Bert Hargrave's JH, Hargrave Mitchell's Half-Diamond M, Eugene Burton's V-T, and to others the brands of which I forget. The owners included P.A. Yeast, Lloyd Tytlandvyk, Rube Gilchrist, Reiny Lehr, Perry Minor, Larry Laidlaw, Henry Cavan, Emerson Porter, Bruce Watson, and others whose names won't come to me now.

Having sons playing for Leslie Cluff's hockey teams from Niblock School kept me busy on Saturday mornings; I was a volunteer driver for outings to Maple Creek, Bow Island, Taber, Brooks, and points in between.

It always interested me that community names would hang on long after there were no physical signs of habitation. In vain did I search for Hoping and Enchant. Residents still used those names for geographic designations, although the communities had vanished.

I developed a new feeling for community one evening when I was asked to speak to a Lions club at a town to the southwest; it may have been Conquerville. Anyway, I got to the appointed spot and found nothing but a community club; nary a house in sight.

Minutes later a pick-up arrived, and a young woman carried a roasting pan into the hall. Then came another with the potato salad, another with the dessert, then the members began arriving, and suddenly the desolation was broken when the building was ringed by half a hundred pickup-trucks and a full-fledged meeting was in progress. In the shortgrass country all you need for a community is the spirit.

My first introduction to irrigation came with a story-writing assignment on farm families relocated to Bow Island from the Yellowgrass district of Saskatchewan. PFRA traded them land, dry stuff for wet stuff. The farmer I wanted to interview wasn't at home, but his wife waved at 160 acres and said, "He's out there someplace...wasn't home all night." I walked the ditches and found him sound asleep beside an irrigation gate, rubber boots on one side of him, shovel on the other.

A great learning experience, this one. This man was raised on a grain farm with its leisurely pace; plant in spring, harvest in fall, no sweat. With irrigation, he had to be on duty literally hour by hour, operating his gates when the ditch rider told him the water was headed his way. For this man to convert to wet farming was a painful conversion.

It was a strange story which took me to Iddesleigh. A number of farm families went on strike, keeping their children out of school to score some political points against their trustees. But the bus driver wouldn't be paid until he drove his allotted mileage, which he did, day after lonely day, week after lonely month all by his lonesome.

On occasion we even went international. The Medicine Hat chamber was invited to tour a missile silo near Great Falls before the warhead was installed. A number of us, I remember Chuck Beny being with us but forget the rest of the names, chartered a small plane for the flight. When we got to the Malmstrom Air Force Base the commandant was curious as to how we had made the trip; our aircraft didn't show on his billion-dollar radar installation.

On the way home we got lost in a blizzard. Our pilot, Bill (last name unknown) flew lower and lower and lower until suddenly he spotted an elevator with the name Seven Persons on its side. He followed the blacktop to the flying field.

On another flight, I left The Hat one morning at dawn in the company of Herman Wahl. Senator Lamontagne wanted to discuss with me my possible appointment to the board of the Canadian Centennial Commission. To keep the appointment, Herman agreed to fly me to Calgary to catch an early-morning flight east. We couldn't land at Calgary because of a downpour, but Herman just flew in circles until he spotted a plane on a farm, then landed in a nearby pasture. The farmer loaned us his brand-new car for the drive to the airport. Just another example of prairie hospitality.

Cypress Club

CYPRESS CLUB: JUST TO SAY THIS NAME OUT LOUD MAKES ME SMILE.

It may be ensconced in the most unprepossessing building on Sixth Street, but do not be deceived. In Medicine Hat, this is the seat of Real Power.

There was a time when I viewed the club as the unofficial headquarters of the Shortgrass Country. If you wanted to get anything done, at any level of government, this was the place to begin.

Go in the front door and you find a centre hallway flanked by small private rooms. That hall leads to the common room which is ringed with chairs. The rule here is the same as in the common room of any university; any conversation being conducted in this area is viewed as being in common. You are expected to participate.

From nine a.m. until midnight, six days a week, the faithful could eat, drink, talk, play pool, play cards, and occasionally make asses of themselves. Ranchers viewed the club as their temporary headquarters in town.

Here they made and received telephone calls, answered mail, and swapped gossip on weather and cattle prices.

For merchants and professionals it was a social headquarters. Many persons visited it several times a day, for coffee breaks, for meals, for the entertainment of out-of-town guests.

The menu was limited, but satisfying. There was always a roast on the go. As you would expect in a ranching community, steaks were a specialty. The cold beef sandwiches were world class.

I can say the same about the chatter. When a dozen members gathered for lunch, and put their minds to work on a single subject, it could be covered exhaustively, from all commercial and philosophic points of view.

Some of the regulars were so attentive in their attendance that they had their own chairs, and we younger ones deferred. Col. Harry Cox faced north; Henry Mitchell faced east; Mack Higdon faced south, always from the same chairs.

As every journalist knows, the majority of news stories are like unborn infants; there is a gestation period. If you were a regular at the club, you were frequently in on major stories as they were developing. It was possible to learn which municipal by-laws were to be amended, which stores or business blocks were in the process of changing hands, who was being transferred and the source of the replacement.

I went to the club for scores of reasons. If I wanted to talk about fund-raising for Fifth Avenue United, I knew where I could find my fellow committee members, Rube Gardner and Russ McBride; at the club. Ditto the stampede and Dirk Scholten and the Fisher brothers; ditto the Shrine club with Pudge McCallum and Red Amos; ditto the chamber of commerce with Chuck Beny and Lorne Tansley.

The general level of decorum was acceptable, but was thrown out the window on "Club Night." Periodically there would be a social evening, and those events added many stories to club lore. One of my favorites concerns the night that lawyer Jimmy Kidd, now Mr. Justice Kidd, took off his neck tie, crawled up on a pool table, lay on his back with his hands folded in front of him, and asked the local funeral director to demonstrate how to tie neckwear on the dear deceased.

In my 10 years of membership two of the stewards were Emil, last name unknown, and everyone's favourite caterer, Robert Gwinner. Faithful servants both, and on occasion, accomplished diplomats. They knew exactly what was expected of them when a member came in and said, "If anyone phones me... I'm not here."

There are memories of great hilarity. One day Robert Gwinner served Dirk Scholten a double helping of curried chicken, and a few moments later asked Dirk if he wanted anything. The big Dutchman could think of only one thing: "Ya, bring me the (censored) fire extinguisher." I one morning wrote in my diary a great line by Bert Hargrave. He said that that day on the JH Ranch things were so dry that the little trees on the river bank were just going from dog to dog!

One morning when I dropped in for coffee I found that a great amount of good-natured banter was being directed at Russ McBride, the manager of Eaton's. Here he was, this popular fellow, all decked out in a new brown suit when everyone else favoured casual slacks and shirtsleeves. Both that suit and its color were up for critical examination.

When I was back at the office I decided to keep the subject alive. I wrote a two-paragraph story, purportedly a dispatch fresh in from overseas. I said that the current edition of *Tailor and Cutter*, England's leading magazine for men's fashions, that week had publicly scolded Prince Philip for appearing in public in a brown suit, a colour suitable only for grouse-shooting. This provided the topic for the coffee break on the following morning, and while I got a suspicious look or two from Russ, he never mentioned it.

Peer Gynt

IT WAS A FRIENDLY VOICE ON THE TELEPHONE, AND THE QUESTION WAS accompanied by a definite chuckle: "Do you remember Peer Gynt?"

The caller was Russ McBride, now long in retirement in Victoria. We're old friends from Medicine Hat where Russ was the manager of Eaton's. It happens on occasion that he will have a flashback so strong that he just has to pick up the telephone so we can chat.

Peer Gynt was a dog, but I insist he was not of the ordinary type. I've written a dozen stories about this unusual creature and his particular attributes: one minute he could do something so remarkable I'd want him as a friend for life; the next moment he'd get into a vexatious mood and try my patience—sorely.

First, a word about his heritage. Peer Gynt, or "Gynt" for short, was a Weimaraner. It was several hundred years ago when the barons of the German province of Weimar decided to breed the master dog. They knew exactly what they wanted in the finished product: it had to have superior eyesight, webbed feet for work in the water, a smooth coat for working in the brambles, and sufficient speed and weight that it could haul down a stag.

In one of my more foolish moves, I decided that I could have a hunting dog that would also be a pet to our four children. After a series of telephone calls, I drove to Calgary and bought a Weimaraner. He was christened Peer Gynt.

There were several sleepless night as we learned how much our new friend really missed his mummy. At this point, Gynt was living in a large wicker basket in a room in the lower level of our home. Across the hall was a bedroom for three little boys. On the first morning when we awoke and realized that our new pet had not kept us awake all night with his howling, I sneaked downstairs and took a peek: Peer Gynt was sound asleep in his basket, but so was Fred Jr.

Because this dog was particularly strong-willed, his training was a challenge. I bought a book titled *Training You to Train Your Dog*. I signed up for obedience classes. I must have walked a thousand miles around the apple trees in our back yard teaching my new friend how to "Come," and "Sit," and "Stay." We finally got to the point at which he would obey these commands—when it suited him.

During this period I was reading everything I could find on the history of the Weimaraner. I learned that due to inbreeding, they had a repeating problem: a number of them were short one of those little orbs which are the symbols of manhood. This raised the obvious question: did we have a complete dog? It took only some rudimentary research for me to learn that—alas—Peer Gynt had only one of what he should have had two of. Oh well, we decided that we wanted a friendly pet and not a show dog so we accepted him into the family, entire or not.

It was on our first outing to the marshes when we learned of another strange characteristic: this was a compulsive retriever. It happened, too frequently, that another hunter, perhaps a half-mile away, would fire his gun and Gynt would see a bird fall from the air. Away he'd go like a racehorse, surmounting all obstacles, as he just had to make that retrieval. We could hear the aggrieved hunter hurling curses to the wind as the dog made his return trip—to us. While my sons thought this was hilarious, there were many adults who did not share in this opinion.

Along with his other compulsions, Gynt was unbelievably possessive. If he thought someone was going to touch something that belonged to me, he would assert himself. It's right here where Russ McBride gets into the picture with one of his favourite memories.

It happened one day that we didn't want the dog with us for some reason, so we left him in the station wagon. When it was time for lunch, Russ volunteered to go and get the car, which was some distance away. He slipped into the driver's seat, he put his hands on the wheel, and then it happened; Gynt put his mouth on Russ's right hand. Not a bite, mind you, just a warning. H-m-m-m.

As you would expect from an Eaton's manager, Russ came up with a solution. He opened the lunch box and took out a sandwich. He rolled down the window, threw the sandwich out, and when the dog went after it, Russ rolled the window up and drove away.

My friend Peer Gynt may have been hard-headed, but he was far from stupid. One summer morning, Fred Jr., and I were walking down a path which leads to the South Saskatchewan River; Gynt was leading the way. Suddenly he stopped, went on extreme alert, then began backing up, ever so slowly.

Only then did we hear the sound... it sounded like dry beans being shaken in a tin cup. Only then did we see what was ahead of us: a rattlesnake, all curled and ready to strike, its upraised tail moving slowly from side to side.

We had many more exploits with Superdog: once we learned that he could chew himself out of most fences, we had to reinforce his pen with heavy wire. We all grieved when it was time for him to go to that so-called happy hunting ground.

But back to Russ's question, Do I remember Peer Gynt? Believe me, I do.

Travel By Train

EVERY TIME I AM ON AN AIRPLANE, ONE DOMINANT THOUGHT rushes to my mind: I wish I could make this trip by train.

I have countless happy memories of travel on those rusty ribbons of steel. I assume this connection springs from my boyhood when Brandon was a major rail centre. At around the time of the outbreak of World War Two, close to half the work force in this community worked for either Canadian Pacific, Canadian National, or the Great Northern.

My oldest train memory is sharp and clear, but not because it was pleasant. It took place during the early '30s, when I was nine or ten. My grandmother and I were traveling from Brandon to Winnipeg on a scorching day in August. Because we were going to a birthday party, we were all dressed up when we got aboard the day coach.

This was in the period before air conditioning. The temperature in that coach was like a Turkish bath. We had not been travelling long before a dreadful dispute arose between some of the passengers. The man in front of us suddenly declared he was going to open a window. There was a chorus of protest that this would fill the coach with dust and cinders. In short, he did and it did. Granny and I looked like coal miners when we arrived.

There have been some sharp changes in travel economics, for which I have proof. When I was a teenager, and the Brandon junior hockey team was in the league finals in Winnipeg, CPR would offer a hockey excursion: a penny a mile. The price for a return ticket, Brandon to Winnipeg, was $2.50. Today this wouldn't pay the taxi that takes you to the depot... if we still had trains, that is.

In the '40s there was an overnight service between Regina and Saskatoon and I was a frequent user. Each evening, around nine, a passenger coach would be located behind the depot in each of those cities. Passengers could get on board between nine and midnight. Some time after that a train connected with that coach and took you to the other city.

One night I got on the coach in Saskatoon, went right to bed and to sleep. Eight hours later I awoke refreshed, convinced that that was the smoothest train trip I had ever made. Then I peeked out the window and noticed that we were still in the Saskatoon depot... there was a broken rail somewhere between those two points.

In those earlier times, when the menu in the average prairie restaurant was far from elegant, having a meal on those old dining cars was our most exciting eating-out experience.

Every evening meal began with a dish of celery and olives. The rolls were so crusty that when you broke one, you sprayed crumbs for six feet around. I can even recall that, on the menu, there was an asterisk beside lamb chops: they took 45 minutes to prepare. They arrived complete with panties.

Oh yes, another oddity. From my office window in Medicine Hat I could see the trains arriving and leaving the CPR depot. One morning I noticed that the CPR *Canadian* arrived at 9:30 instead of ten. I knew enough about train lore to know this is not supposed to happen. I called the depot and got the word from the agent: "That's not today's *Canadian*...that's yesterday's!"

I had a close connection with the *Canadian*. In those days before air travel, I used it four times a year for trips to Toronto for the Southam company. My friend Basil Dean, publisher of the *Calgary Herald*, who was going to the same meetings, would get on board in Calgary, and I would do the same in Medicine Hat. Each of us had a bag of books. For two days and two nights we would sleep, and read, and chat in that order.

Especially memorable was a trip that Christine and I once made from Medicine Hat to Vancouver and back.

The CPR superintendent in The Hat, William Flett, was summoned to the coast. He was to be a witness in a corporate lawsuit. He decided to take his private car, and company was invited.

There was Bill's wife Mary, and Bert and Amy Hargrave, and Christine and me. There was a compartment for each couple. And a private chef. And a well-stocked larder. That coach was hooked on to the back of a fast freight.

Let me say that I don't care how fast an airplane can go, for sheer elegance, nothing will ever match travel in a private car. And now, alas, I can't even get a ride in an old-fashioned day coach.

That trip even had moments of high drama. Two or three times, when we were leaving the station in Calgary, Superintendent Flett reminded his chef that, at the west end of the yards, there is a machine that washes passengers coaches as they pass by.

Alas, the chef forgot these instructions. He left his window open. I can still recall those shouts of rage when the car wash sprayed both chef and galley with hot, soapy water.

A.M. Pennie, Esq.

LET ME TELL YOU ABOUT A MEMORABLE OBSERVATION ON A BEAUTIFUL morning in July of 1964. It took place in southern Alberta.

I stood on a hilltop on the Suffield research station in the company of a score of journalists. We faced west. The most dominant object in sight was a mound of brown stuff the size of a three-storey house. It was on another hill, several miles away.

In a shallow valley between those two hilltops were some objects strangely out of place for this prairie setting: I recognized the bow structure of a warship. There were parts of aircraft. There were rows of telephone poles, even brick walls at various angles. We could see trenches in which mannequins wore various protective articles of clothing. There were many more things we journalists were not allowed to know about.

Soon there was a dramatic countdown, and the first sign of action was the firing of a series of rockets, then BOOM!!!! What happened right then was the largest man-made explosion in Canadian history.

Now, there's a particular reason to tell you this story right now, 32 years later. The other day I picked up a newspaper and there was the picture of the man who pushed the button for that Big Blast.

There he was: Archibald Munro Pennie, now in retirement from his last federal post—deputy chairman of the Defense Research Board.

When we knew each other he was the superintendent of the Defense Research Station at Suffield, Alberta, north of Medicine Hat.

What puts friend Archie into the news columns these days is a new federal publication: "Defense Research Establishment Valcartier: 50 years of History and Scientific Progress."

At Suffield, in the early '60s, there was a research program under way to determine the extent of the damage that an atomic bomb would create. It was decided to simulate such a blast. The best way to describe this project is to say it was overwhelming in size. The explosion would involve 450 tonnes of TNT. To measure the extent of the damage, there were literally countless artifacts located at various distances from ground zero.

A group of journalists was invited to be observers, along with 400 scientists from Canada, Australia, Great Britain, and the United States.

As soon as I read the story about Archie Pennie and the big blast, I looked up at a large color picture on my wall: this is a shot of the blast. In the lower right-hand corner are the vapor trails of those rockets. They are all curving, to reflect the effects of that explosion.

The ground shook. We could see the shock wave approaching, for it pressed the grass down as it moved. We were not knocked over, but certainly we buffeted about. I cannot describe the dimensions of the ball of fire that followed the blast; just let me say it was immense. As it proceeded heavenward it assumed that familiar mushroom shape.

And then it was over, at least for the observers. I'm certain that Dr. Pennie and his fellow scientists spent months writing the details of the damage done to their ground monitors. That may have been the conclusion of the big blast, but not of my association with Dr. A.M. Pennie. He doesn't know this, but he is my model of the individual who views life as a learning project.

One day we both abandoned our respective offices in order to take part in a pheasant hunt. From early morning until mid-afternoon we prowled the irrigation ditches. At the time of our afternoon stand-easy, Archie asked me for the time. I said it was four o'clock. He then said he'd soon have to get home; he had a welding class tonight at the junior college. I asked the obvious question: why would a senior scientist want that course. He said he signed up for a course every winter, and this year it just happened to be welding.

Oh yes, let me not forget that the man who pushed the button for that big blast at Suffield, once gave me a demonstration of the lesser variety.

On the day we travelled by air from Calgary to Ottawa, Archie Pennie asked me if I'd like to ride to my hotel in his cab. I said yes.

The wheels had not even begun to roll when Dr. Pennie told the driver to throw his cigarette out the window. The driver had a ready response: this was his cab and he would smoke if he felt like it.

Archie Pennie then responded by saying that the driver might own it, but he had put it under lease to his passengers, who now controlled it, environment and all. This exchange continued until the driver rolled down his window, thew his smoke out the window, and settled down in a surly silence.

Ever since that exchange, I've always wished I had the nerve to do what friend Archie did.

The Detection Of Lies

Now, I'm certain that all of you will remember what Lord Byron said about the truth. No? Well, let me refresh your memories. In *Don Juan*, he wrote "'tis strange, but true; for truth is always strange—stranger than fiction."

In that quiet period between Christmas and New Year's I was working on some notes for the journalism class at Brandon U. Because I needed some actual case histories which tell how stories evolve, I told them a story which, I think, proves His Lordship's point: truth is stranger than fiction.

Early one morning, and early in the sixties, I was at my desk at the *Medicine Hat News* when the telephone rang. It was one of the directors of the local consumer co-operative.

He asked for a favour: something had occurred they did not want to read about in the news columns. After some delay the reason for the call was divulged, and a most remarkable story it was.

The day previous, the co-op had had a major sale. It coincided with the opening of their new premises, and in every respect it had been a smasher. At day's end, they tallied up the results and found themselves facing a major problem: while the new store was open, it wasn't quite finished. The door had not arrived for the vault.

Here comes a question that may daunt the most imaginative of you: Assume with me that you have had a great day at the store, and you're sitting looking at $60,000 in cash and cheques. Assume further that you have no vault, and in this period, there were no night depositories. Here comes the big question: what do you do with that money?

Well, in Medicine Hat the store management had an idea for which I give them full marks: they called the police station and begged an indulgence; they explained the situation, and asked that a suitcase containing all this booty be locked in a cell until Monday morning. They made this request of a co-operative desk sergeant and within the hour the money was under lock and key. Thus endeth part one of this story.

Part two begins at three o'clock the next morning when a masked man burst into the police station, revolver in hand, and forced the duty officer to hand over the key to the cell. Masked man and loot were soon out of sight. This is the story that the board of directors did not want to read about. Needless to say they did, and so did the rest of Canada. This was a front-page story for weeks.

The chief of police was known as John Bull. Actually his first name was Arundel, but John seemed more appropriate. This was a former Mountie, a man who was widely known as slow moving, and deliberate in the extreme. It was his patience and thoroughness which solved this crime.

One of the first things he did was to call in, from Chicago, an expert with the lie detector. Because I was writing reams about this story, Chief Bull suggested that I take the test; it would give me a sidebar to the seamier side of things.

At the appointed hour I reported to a room in the Assiniboia Hotel for an unforgettable experience. A friendly fellow hooked me up with electrodes on my arms, wrists, and chest. The test began with questions so innocuous that I thought this was a piece of cake: Do you ever eat chocolate? Do you eat it once a week? Do you have a preference between apples and oranges? Who is your favorite movie star? Have you bought a jazz record recently? I was sailing right along—no sweat—and then he zapped me with a zinger:

HAVE YOU EVER IN YOUR LIFE STOLEN ANYTHING?

Heavens, what a question: was he talking about Mrs. Pope's plums? Mrs. Neill's carrots? The peanut brittle I lifted when my mother was making candy for a church sale? Or, that day at sea, when a couple of us stole a pie from the galley?

I hemmed and hawed on that one, as well as with some peripheral questions concerning the problem at the cop shop.

When my test was over, and I thanked the technician for the experience, I suddenly realized that I was terribly tired and drenched with perspiration.

Well, let me give full credit to Chief Bull; he solved the crime. It was a member of the force who was convicted and who went to prison. Things eventually returned to normal, and soon the relationship between the newspaper and the co-op was as harmonious as ever.

A.Y. Jackson

ONE RECENT AFTERNOON I WAS PROWLING THROUGH THE SHELVES in a bookstore and I saw a Group of Seven pictorial calendar. This triggered a memory of the week in which I had not one, but two, chats with one of those great artists.

Now, I cannot tell you this story without providing the background. This is going to take a minute.

In 1957, when I was at the *Medicine Hat News*, the Southam company asked me if I would care to attend a session at the Banff School of Advanced Management. They wanted to send an employee and get some feedback on the educational process. I was a cheerful volunteer, and away I went for the six-week live-in course of training in that mountain vastness.

Before I get to the artistic part of this commentary, I must tell you something about my fellow scholars. We were 92 in number. The dominant group came from British Columbia. They had a simplistic view of the world: they divided the class into two categories: east-slopers and west-slopers. You were a west-sloper if you lived west of the Rockies. Otherwise you were an east-sloper, and hence—in this myopic view—a decidedly inferior person.

Again in this view, the only hope for an east-sloper was to move across that range of rocks. If this happened, there would be a magical transformation to your status in life. At least, that was the theory.

Oh yes, about the training. It was by way of a series of case studies. In the evening we read the details of corporate problems as outlined in our textbooks; the next day we had to take a position on the solutions to those problems.

The rules of the Banff School were quite specific: each class had to have some officers. Through a process I never understood, I ended up as vice-president. A member of the administration patiently explained my job to me: I was to collect money from each student and buy a gift for the school.

Collecting that money really was not a problem: I decided that $10 per head was a nice round sum, for surely $920 would buy a gift of lasting value. My fellow students were co-operative. Between the president and myself we agreed that I should try to buy a painting.

After a brief consultation with the artistic types at the school, I learned that there was a member of the Group of Seven still living—and still painting. His name was A.Y. Jackson. He lived in Toronto.

To my astonishment this man's name was in the telephone book, and to my greater surprise—he answered the telephone himself.

Well, I explained that I had this money and that I needed a painting right away. I calculated that I could spend $800 for the artistic work and save the rest for transportation, framing, and the appropriate brass plaque.

After I told my story this great artist told me how sorry he was that—at that moment—he had nothing to sell.

Then there was a moment of silence, and then came the question, asked tentatively... How much money did you say you had?

I repeated... eight hundred dollars.

At this point there was another pause and then came the joyful news: Mr. Jackson said that while he had nothing right then—he would have something by the end of the week! He asked me to call him the next Saturday.

I did as I was asked. This time he told me he was just wrapping the painting and he would send it to me via railway express. It arrived a few days later and I must tell you that I had a little trouble getting it unwrapped: It had been packaged while still damp.

In the intervening 40 years I had completely forgotten the name of the picture; I couldn't even recall what it depicted.

Last week I called the Banff School for some details. Art curator Catherine Crowston was not available for a telephone call, but one of her associates was most helpful. John Burril told me that the painting is "Georgian Bay, October," and he describes it as "a landscape with autumn colours of purple, red and yellow."

And there you have my story. Some day I will tell my grandchildren that I once purchased an A.Y. Jackson original for eight hundred dollars, and that today, at auction, it is worth a king's ransom.

What I won't tell them is that I'm still kicking myself; I should have bought one for myself at the same time. Why didn't I? For about eight hundred reasons.

The Captain Keeps His Promise

THERE WAS A PERIOD IN THE EARLY '60S WHEN A GROUP OF HATTERS engaged in a series of social functions which can best be described as frenzied.

There were house parties and ranch parties. There were barbecues and skating parties. Occasionally there would be privately-sponsored parties as often as three nights in a row at the Assiniboia Hotel. There were parties on New Year's Eve which initially went from house to house but eventually became so large that they were re-located to the Shrine Club. The first Shrine clubroom was nothing more than a large empty space over Red Amos's garage. The second was a wartime hut across from the airport.

For a brief period we turned the fabled "Hat hospitality" into a commercial undertaking. The Shriners had a large set of barbecue grills which we used for club socials. It wasn't long before we were catering meals for groups of visitors, such as the stockgrowers. I thought it helpful to ecumenicity that one year we catered a convention of the Knights of Columbus.

While there have been a million lies told about the Medicine Hat weather, I am prepared to attest to one climactic event which I now write up for the history book. Late one New Year's Eve a chinook blew in with such intensity that it turned the Shrine-club parking lot into a sea of slop. For many of us, the only answer to the problem of wives with unprotected dancing slippers was to carry our partners from parked vehicle to building portal.

But, not for nothing does "Hat" weather have a reputation for changeability. In that lengthy period between our arrival and departure, probably from nine to three, a cold front replaced the chinook, and half of us had our cars frozen into parking-lot mud.

A social event of national interest took place early one summer at the JH ranch at Walsh. Bert Hargrave and Amy were host and hostess to Bert's wartime buddies and their descendants, yea into several generations.

This represents one of the extremely few times in my journalistic career when I have willingly played the role of censor. News personnel allegedly hate censorship more than the devil hates holy water, according to social legend, but there are times when the rules have to be bent.

Bert Hargrave during World War Two was officer commanding a mobile tank-repair outfit. It became a regimental joke that the captain while on civvy street operated a gopher ranch. When peace broke out and the outfit disbanded, Bert's farewell speech included an offer that some day he'd stage a reunion.

At that time *Weekend Magazine* was a popular weekly newspaper insert, and I had to attend periodic meetings of the magazine's board of directors. When I mentioned at one of them that a rancher was going to put up a couple of hundred visitors under canvas, I was assigned to write the story. Bert and Amy were happy to co-operate, but there was a condition; they didn't want any reunion stories to appear in the *Medicine Hat News* because they simply couldn't handle any more visitors. *Weekend Magazine*? Well, that was okay, because it wouldn't appear until several weeks after the reunion broke up.

Did you ever read the story of Gargantua, a character in the writings of Rabelais? He was a legendary Celtic character known for his appetite? You'd have thought he was coming for tea at the JH if you knew what Amy did in preparation.

She baked the buns, the pies, and the bread sufficient for 200-plus visitors who were staying half a week. Every batch was loaded into an orange crate and delivered to the freezer plant on South Railway. Every morning of the reunion she called me at breakfast time and put in that day's order, "Two boxes of blueberry pies, two boxes of apple pies, four boxes of buns... " I was the delivery boy. I spent each day at the reunion visiting with returned men and their families present from ten provinces. *Weekend Magazine* published the story under the heading, "The Captain Keeps His Promise."

Another notable social event was staged on the spur of the moment by Bert's cousin Hargrave Mitchell. Early one winter a small lake on the Half-Diamond M. froze in the complete absence of snow. No factory-new mirror ever had a smoother surface.

What to do? Well, get on the telephone with a come-one-come-all invitation. There must have been 10-15 carloads of us responded, including many who hadn't been on skates for years. Somewhere in the pictures waiting to be sorted are a few which show a crack-the-whip line which would run from the Finlay Bridge to the old city hall. The motive power was Hargrave Mitchell's Volkswagen. For a week afterward every step was painful, but there were no complaints. Never before in my life had I been on a skating surface which ran a couple of miles in every direction.

The Unforgettable Harry Veiner

LET ME DRAW YOU A WORD PICTURE.

It is 5:55 on a July morning. I hurry down the hallway of our home on 12th Street SW to put on the coffee. Just as I am about to turn into the kitchen I see a strange sight; a man is standing on the driveway, peering into the picture window.

This is a large man who is wearing a large hat. It is His Worship, Mayor Harry Veiner. He is waiting to see if the paving crew working on our street reports for duty on time at six.

This was fairly typical of the man known across several provinces as just "Harry." He ran Medicine Hat as if he owned all the shares. There was no aspect of civic work into which he would not venture, from investing the pre-paid taxes to debating the diameter of sewer lines. It wasn't easy for the city supervisors to work for him; he was much too impatient to go through bureaucratic channels.

I have written many stories about this unusual man, and when I think about them I think of the conundrum he represents, one to which I have never found the answer: either he has a secret source of information on a global basis, or else he has a seventh sense.

In agriculture, Harry Veiner was a genuine leader. By the time the farmers had concluded that there was an expanding market for rye, he was getting out of it and switching to another crop. By the time the chicken farmers had converted to turkeys because of a pending shortage, he had shipped his last load of toms. His perspicacity was such that he could sniff out developing markets and work them to his advantage.

There will be many people who do not know how big or how soft this man's heart can be—on occasion. He was visiting me one evening when three little boys came down the hall to "kiss Daddy goodnight." When they had done so I was surprised to see the tears coursing down Harry's face; while he loved his two daughters dearly, he had always wanted a son. This was the same man who could be a tiger in an argument if he believed that someone was trying to get the better of him.

On a fairly regular basis he would call and invite me to spend a day in the country with him. This meant he wanted to visit his holdings of ranches, grain farms, and dairy farms, or look at another property he heard was coming on the market.

Stop for lunch? Never. I've seen him go into a store at Irvine or Brooks and buy a loaf of bread and a chunk of summer sausage. We would eat on the go, tearing away at the victuals in the style of Henry the Eighth. Time is money.

He was capable of quixotic actions. One evening coming home from Calgary he stopped at the farm near Brooks which bears his name emblazoned on the barn roof. I waited in the car as Harry tore a strip off the farmer for burning too many lights. I was in his company at 4-H auctions when he would work the bid for the champion steer up to an astronomical level, then quit, leaving a packer or retailer to pay up. When I was chairman of the United Fund, Harry always held back his donation until the campaign was near the end; he wanted to put it over the top. This was fine with me for that gift always was generous.

Meetings of council committees were held in his office at city hall, and today I wish I had a video of one of them. He sat with his back to the Sixth Street wall; city clerk Bill Keith sat in one corner and city-hall reporter McGuinness sat in the other. Councilors ringed the wall; Gust, Scott, McComb, Heckbert, Gibson, Simpson, Osborne, Sissons, Lutes, Adam, or some combination of these. The debate was always punctuated by Harry's telephone calls; he bought land, sold turkeys, appeased dissidents, and argued with his broker, all without missing the thread of conversation.

Harry loved publicity, of the good type. "Don't wait 'til I'm dead before you send me flowers," was a frequent refrain. When The Hat in the late '60s suffered a shortage of tradesmen he thought this was worthy of some national publicity. He asked me for a hand.

A long-time friend of mine was the late Stan Obodiac, PR man for Maple Leaf Gardens. I called Stan, told him the story, and he arranged for Harry to be a guest on the Hockey Night in Canada hot-stove league. A week later we flew east from Calgary.

Harry gave a stellar performance. The plan was that this would be a cameo appearance, two or three minutes at best, but the organizers didn't know our Harry. When he got that microphone in his hand, and an audience of millions hanging on every word, he wouldn't quit until he'd told the story the way he wanted; Medicine Hat's economy was so buoyant that there was a shortage of people. A week later CBC television asked me to tell the same story on an afternoon show hosted by Fred Davis. Only recently I came across a packet of mail from tradesmen asking for more information. I'm donating them to the Medicine Hat archives.

Harry Veiner is worthy of a major biography. After all, can you name another person who has cut sugar cane with Fidel Castro?, beat a racehorse in a 25-yard dash?, and played on the line with the Saskatchewan Roughriders? I think not. Even in a territory known for its characters, he's one of a kind.

Medicine Hat Council Notes

YOU DO NOT REQUIRE A PH.D. IN POLITICAL SCIENCE TO KNOW THE traditional relationship between the journalist and the politician; they make the cobra and the mongoose look like sorority sisters.

When Bill Hogle was editor of *The News*, he viewed city hall as his private assignment, and no other staffer ever even visited there, except at Bill's vacation time. He loved the political life. For him council coverage was never a chore.

He even—once at least—made some journalistic history, of sorts. When he lacked the facts for a council story, he just settled down behind his typewriter and made up the yarn out of his head, the way he felt council should have performed.

It was Simon Scott who put me on to this odd caper. The alderman telephoned me at home in the first week of May to complain about a story in that evening's edition. He insisted that it was not at all correct, and how could it be, he questioned; it was written by someone who was not present.

This amounted to a serious complaint, and so in the morning I visited Bill in his office. It didn't take the story long to emerge, for he was filled with remorse. He was just about to enter city hall for the council meeting in question when "Red" Amos drove by. They fell to visiting, and the result was that one of them bought a bottle of gin and they drank it while sitting on the top row of seats in the stampede grandstand. They called this the ushering in of the of "Summer gin season."

After Bill left the paper I became the city-hall reporter. The relationship with the councilors was really quite good, but when the periodic fallings-out occurred, they could be severe. Some of the councilors had been badly spoiled. Occasionally they would ask that something be kept out of the paper, and in an earlier period this had been done. I thought then this was unacceptable journalism, and still do.

The result was that on occasion we'd get into a scrap. To retaliate against the paper, the aldermen would meet ahead of the regular session, determine where they stood on each issue, and then in the public meeting, move and second their motions without debate. I can remember occasional evenings when it took us only 18 minutes to go from opening to adjournment.

Medicine Hat never had an elected representative who took the duties more seriously than Helen Beny Gibson. She made many accomplishments for the electorate, and none of them came easily. Mrs. Gibson was not only well educated, but also she was deadly serious.

This faithful public servant wanted to apply logic to situations where logic is a foreigner, i.e. in the council committees when politics is both king and queen and where logic has no natural home. Despite our occasional differences, she was always welcome in my office; she was so well organized that when she telephoned in advance, asking for a two-minute appointment, I knew she meant exactly what she said.

Did I have a favorite alderman? If so, it was Edgar McComb. There was a connection between us so thin as to be almost invisible; when Edgar was a student railroader, my grandfather was the conductor who supervised him.

However, even a three-generation connection is no guarantee of harmony in politics. Once when we fell into disagreement on some issue, I wrote an editorial which criticized Edgar for his stand. At the next council meeting he rose to make a statement. That editorial, in his opinion, reminded him of the story of the farmer who'd been kicked by a jackass. "It doesn't hurt nearly as much when you consider the source!"

There must have been a period in which I didn't have nearly enough to do; I found the time to write some doggerel. In a council battle over whether to issue a building permit for a new apartment block, I came down solidly on the side of Ald.

Helen Gibson. My ode, if I may call it that, was a parody of "Curfew Shall Not Ring Tonight."

'Twas the afternoon of Monday, 'twas the day that council met,
Helen sat at home and pondered, brow all furrowed, lips grim set,
Could she win the fight, she wondered, could she stall that last decree?
"Damn those rude apartment builders! Damn their enterprise so free!"
She would not give up, she knew it; she had just begun to fight,
Then she breathed the husky whisper,
"COUNCIL MUST NOT VOTE TONIGHT!"

If you think that's bad, you should read the rest; it goes on for half a mile. I will never know what prompted it, but 30 years later I'm prepared to defend it for what it is; a slightly off-centre show of respect for a woman who was a two-fisted battler.

Canadian Pacific

It was a matter of special interest to me that Medicine Hat was an exclusive spot for the CPR; this reinforced my inherited bias.

My family had an assortment of associations with the "National Dream." My father and mother in an earlier era both worked for the express service; my mother was the first female to work in the Brandon depot. Grandpa was a conductor. A sister and I both worked for CP Telegraphs.

When I arrived in The Hat, the influence of those rusty ribbons of steel, as early historians called them, was pervasive. Those of us who were high-mileage travellers came and went via passenger trains. The arrival of company meant trips to the CP depot. Eddie Rutherford would smile at me from his window in the ticket department. He one day told me he'd just sent a local couple to Hawaii on a budget plan, "For two weeks on the sand they get two years on the rocks."

My affinity for CPR was reinforced by friendship with a variety of superintendents, and the regular visits of railway vice-presidents. For the chamber annual meeting, or during Stampede Week, we could count on the support of senior rail men like Arthur McCallum Fraser, the regional VP. When we learned that my mother-in-law had attended school in the company of his wife, he claimed what he described as the thinnest of associations, "Our relatives had hung out their laundry under the same sun."

As a CP loyalist I demanded nothing but the best of service, and almost always received it. Note that qualifier.

I got on board *The Canadian* one evening en route to Brandon and the funeral of a sister. In the morning when I took my shoes out of the shoe container in the bedroom, I made a stunning discovery; one shoe was definitely mine; the other was two sizes too small. With only a brief station stop and no porter in sight there was nothing for me to do but don my slippers and scuff my way to the nearest shoe store.

By this time my dander was up. From the telegraph office I dispatched a lengthy missive to superintendent W.R. Flett, Esquire, telling him that both his and his employer's reputations were in jeopardy. One day later and the divisional chief clerk made a personal delivery of the missing footwear.

But this is kid stuff compared with the strangest railway story in which I ever became involved.

I was on my way back from Toronto on *The Canadian,* scheduled to arrive in The Hat at about 9:30 on a Sunday morning. My wake-up call was listed in the porter's book. Surprise! When I awoke the train had been through town and was heading west up the Redcliff hill. An apologetic sleeping-car conductor promised he'd let me off at Suffield. From there I telephoned home and a rescue mission was organized.

One day later and the plot thickens. I sat next to Bill Flett at Rotary, and he's not his usual cheery self; he has a mystery on his hands. One of Bill's neighbors was driving down the Trans-Canada on Sunday morning and saw *The Canadian* stop at Suffield, not a regular event. He told Bill about it. Bill called the train crew to his office and to a man they swore that the train never stopped. This was the union brethren protecting that porter from discipline.

No Cheshire cat ever smiled more broadly. After extracting a promise of non-retribution, I told him the story. He had trouble believing how small the world can be, and so do I, even these 30 years later.

It was that same William Flett who one day decided he should inspect a lot of track between Bassano and Empress. Being a social pragmatist, he decided the means of inspection should be from a pair of jiggers loaded with hunters and shotguns; this was the opening of the pheasant season.

A half dozen of us were Bill's guests the previous evening on his private car in the Bassano yards. After dinner we fell to gossiping about changes in the transportation system. As we talked about evolution I divulged for the first time that in the '40s I had been a press operator for CP Telegraphs, and that over the course of a few years in pre-teletype days I'd worked on CP's behalf at both the *Winnipeg Tribune* and the *Winnipeg Free Press.*

Well, the reaction was total disbelief. When I offered to put my talents to the test I was offered a rash of wagers, all of which I accepted. We all walked over the rails to the depot, where yes, a co-operative agent had a handful of telegrams to be dispatched to Calgary. He loaned me his "bug." I sent them. I collected the bets.

It would be 10 years later when Bill Flett reminded me what a thoughtful gentleman he could be. One day on my desk at the *Brandon Sun* I found a large, awkward package; this was an old-fashioned telegraph sounder and relay system, which I still treasure. Somewhere on Bill's trackage a crew was dismantling a depot and he rescued for me these reminders of the "olden times" when distance communication called for dots and dashes.

All Hell For A Basement

MEDICINE HAT. JUST THINKING OF THE NAME CAUSES THE MEMORIES to flow, just like the South Saskatchewan, alongside which I laboured for 10 delightful years.

Medicine Hat. This makes me think of the crowd in the Hat Hardware on a Saturday afternoon. There are ranchers in plum-coloured stetsons, insulated vests, jeans, and fancy cowboy shoes. They talk about the calf crop and how nice it would be to have an inch of rain.

Medicine Hat. This makes me think of the day I came out of the side door of Eaton's and saw a sign across the street which read, "BAKEREI UND KONDITOREI." That spelling may be shaky, but my smattering of German left over from college told me this was a bakery and confectionery. Indeed it was, and a great line of diet-defying goodies it dished out. This was my introduction to the German influence.

Medicine Hat. This makes me think of Baptiste Carnelli whirling around his tiny shop like a dervish. He always wore a tiny leather cap of the type the East Indians call a "Nehru." He always smiled.

Medicine Hat. This makes me think of merchants squabbling with city council over summer shopping hours. At the newspaper we took the position that there's no need for a shopping-hours by-law, that a merchant who has invested in an inventory should be able to offer it to the public at will, all night long, if that's the wish.

One year the retailers voted to close on Wednesday afternoon; and almost all of those who voted yes were fibbing when they cast their ballots. What they did was play charades. What happened on the next Wednesday? They had no lights on. There were no apparent signs of life. But those of us who were curious about these things always found that the front door was open. We could go from Hawthorne's to Hutching's to Raber's to wherever and in each shop we'd find the proprietor in the back, waiting for us. Oh, he was only doing the books, as he explained it, but he wouldn't mind playing a symphony on his cash register if we wanted to buy something.

Medicine Hat. This reminds me of driving visitors through Police Point, which always reminded me of a scene from Disney's Fantasia. Scores of droughts over a century or more had resulted in this collection of misshapen cottonwoods which had overseen the development of a community from Indian battleground to thriving industrial centre.

Medicine Hat. This conjures up a thousand memories. Let me conclude with one of lasting value.

It was Dr. Noel (I forget his last name) who recruited me to be chairman of a college-library fund. He had an agreement from Premier Manning that if we could come up with the money for the basic library, the college could offer first-year credit courses.

The objective? $30,000. My partner in the collections? Eugene Burton. We agreed that all we needed was 30 gifts of $1,000 each. His was first.

In only a couple of weeks we went from farm to factory, from ranch to Calgary executive suite. In each case I introduced the subject, and then Gene bore in with the heavy message. His central theme? He hated large universities in far-off places. "They take country kids and turn them into city kids, and we never get them back again. We need a local college so we can keep our kids at home."

This may sound to you like a strange sales pitch, but it worked. In two weeks we had the money. That library put the college into business.

Medicine Hat. This makes me think of a tiny delegation in my office. Three women want to know if I'll pour tea at a social in honor of St. Patrick's Day. One of these daughters of Erin is Mrs. Schlinker, the second is Mrs. Schlenker, the third is Mrs. Schaufele.

Medicine Hat. This makes me think of an unusual collection of cultural talent. One month we could go to the Towne and see local players in a spirited performance of *Annie Get Your Gun,* or *Seven-And-A-Half-Cents,* or *Brigadoon*; the next we were running around town raising money to send the local players to the Dominion Drama Festival. If you turned Rod Ashburner and Noreen Flanagan loose on a project, the sky was the limit.

Medicine Hat. This reminds me of friend Dave Broadfoot on TV, standing for office on the grounds that if he were elected, he'd bring big activity to the "Forgotten Corner." I say the only people who forget The Hat are those who have never lived there.

Medicine Hat. The community with all hell for a basement has all heaven for a heart.

Brandon

An Earlier Brandon Sun

"SORRY, FRED, BUT WE DON'T DO THINGS LIKE THAT." I DIDN'T believe this response when I heard it 35 years ago, and I still don't believe it today.

When I returned to Brandon, after a 25-year absence, the *Brandon Sun* was in one of its super-conservative modes. As I was getting to know the crew, and the corporate culture, I often wondered how it would be possible to effect the changes I was supposed to make without upsetting everyone in the process. In Medicine Hat, at *The News*, I had been too hasty when I attempted to amend some hoary old practices. I learned then how important it is to determine the rate at which change will be accepted.

What elicited that troublesome response was a suggestion I made to the news desk. A man had died recently, and I knew that as a teen-ager, in the war in France, he had been awarded the Military Medal. I felt then—and still do—that this was a human-interest story worth pursuing. When I was told "we don't do things like that," it was explained to me that this would be selective news coverage, that it wouldn't be fair to make a precedent and tell the story of one individual when we had to overlook many others.

I demurred. I said my suggestion would be a perfect precedent which could apply every time there was another teener who was honoured for "conspicuous gallantry in the face of the enemy." I didn't make a sale, and in my newness I decided it wasn't wise to press the point.

So, I went back upstairs and pondered. This wasn't the first time I knew *The Sun* had passed over stories that I believed were worthy of coverage. As I reflected, I decided that if I couldn't go over the top of the mountain, I would go around it. I decided to write a local column, something I had done for years in Medicine Hat.

At that time, as the new boy on the street, I didn't want it to appear under my own name. I looked out my office window at the corner of Fifth and Rosser, and a low-grade inspiration struck: F.A. Rosser it would be. Thus, F.A. Rosser became a columnist.

At the outset, what I specialized in was local news that the newsroom, at that time, chose to ignore. When some changes were effected in the lower level, and that old super-conservative mode passed away, I ventured into other fields: trip reports, book reviews, interviews with former residents... just about anything that came to mind.

Newspapers are forever receiving strange requests, many of them asking for assistance in finding lost or missing relatives. This led me into a few really interesting stories in which old mysteries were solved with the help of *Sun* subscribers.

"My name is Horace Logan. I live in Thief River Falls, Minnesota. I hear you help people who are looking for long-lost kinfolk." This was the genesis for one of these requests.

The missing party was an ageing bachelor who had farmed for many years in the Rounthwaite district. His nephew hadn't heard from him for 25 years and wondered if Uncle was still in these parts. I published the request.

Bingo! Three times in one weekend I received anonymous telephone calls suggesting that I stop this search right now. Calls of this type are nothing more than journalistic catnip; I pressed on with a new motivation. There was plenty of news once I found a few willing sources.

The bachelor had been a strange one. He not only lived alone, but he wanted it this way. Those few persons who had gained admittance to his small shack had been intrigued to see that the walls were covered with colour pictures cut out of those old rotogravure tabloids.

What my original informant did not know was that those colour pictures all featured the evangelist, famous in that period, Aimee Semple McPherson. One autumn, after harvest, the bachelor told his neighbour he was going to California to meet the lady. Before long he had returned to Rounthwaite where he sold land, equipment, and cattle, and this time he told the neighbour he was going to California again, this time to marry the reverend (?) lady. In the spring he came home again, unmarried, destitute, and he had to be committed to the mental health centre, where he died.

After all of this, which involved numerous interviews and telephone calls, there was nothing to do but become the courier of sad tidings. I gave Horace Logan the details. He thanked me warmly for my detective work and concluded our conversation by stating that "It's reassuring to know that the poor old bugger had some human impulses."

We faced an unusual challenge one day in the '70s. I learned about it at 3 a.m. when Don Ready telephoned me to say that the folder on the press had smashed, and we wouldn't be able to publish that day. At the office a few minutes later there was a meeting of Ready, Lyle Macson, and me.

We divided up the duties. I telephoned Rick Derksen at the *Steinbach Carillon* and opened negotiations. Ready and Macson began to re-schedule work on that day's edition of *The Sun* in order that the pages could be trucked to Steinbach for printing. As I recall it we had some papers by eight p.m. that evening, and we published in this manner for three days. One challenge faced—one challenge met.

Because my connection with *The Sun* ran over a hard-to-believe 60 years, I knew quite a bit about its history. In my messenger days it was under the iron control of editor W.H. Noakes, who had an unusual blend of talents: he was a journalist, cartoonist, and humourist, and good at all three. Under his direction, for many years *The Sun* was proclaimed annually as Canada's "most quoted newspaper."

The basis of this unusual honour was a daily feature called Sun Gleams. These were mini-editorials, mainly one-liners, in which a man with an acid wit commented on the major stories and personalities of the day. Noakes could do more damage to reputations with 18 words than most editorial writers could do in that many paragraphs. One day he told me he'd been instructed to write an editorial lamenting the death of someone he could not stand. As he explained it, "I have been ordered to write what I call a son-of-a-bitchuary."

Corporate Communications

A WHILE AGO, IN A CHAT WITH A YOUNG REPORTER, OUR CONVERSATION wandered onto the subject of local persons in high places.

Should the newspaper announce local appointments? Should executive changes at a local institution be acknowledged? Does the public care who is in charge of what school, or store, or corporation? From my observation, this is a matter of local option, and the rules are changing rapidly. I can attest to this from my experience on small dailies.

Forty years ago, on the *Medicine Hat News*, it was standard practice to announce major changes of leadership. A new principal at the high school would be acknowledged with a head-and-shoulders picture, and a brief biography. If a new bank manager came to town—ditto.

In those days we had rigid pecking orders in the business community. The manager of the T. Eaton Company was at the pinnacle. I have worked in towns that viewed him as the Pope of Main Street. At a meeting of the chamber of commerce he announced what his store hours were going to be, and that usually set them for the whole community.

Well, friends, there have been changes in what I call executive identification. They seem to have gone underground. Today I do not know the name of the manager of the nearest Eaton's store, nor did I know the one before that, or the one before that.

I am certain that competitors like K-Mart, and Zeller's, and Wal-Mart have general managers, but I have never seen one, met one, nor have I heard their names. I suspect they sneak into town on the midnight bus and remain underground.

As for me, I have a strong preference for corporate leaders who have a presence, and make it known, and who have the courage to make comments on current issues. I view them as real leaders.

From my days in Medicine Hat I can give you an idea of what I mean. I was busy on the keyboard one day when my secretary came in and laid a business card on my desk. She said, "He's waiting to see you."

I read the card. It said, "Ronald Todgham, president, Chrysler Canada." I had trouble believing my eyes, so I asked my helper for confirmation. "Do you mean he's waiting for me?" She assured me that yes, the Chrysler president was cooling his heels in the outer office.

Thus began a memorable meeting. Mr. President was on a national tour, wandering in and out of towns on a non-scheduled basis. He told me that he had trouble believing his ad agency personnel, and some of his executives, most of whom were interested in telling the big chief what they thought he wanted to hear.

To get the straight goods from the marketplace, he found it instructive to wander into a community and do nothing more complicated than just ask questions. He asked barbers, and taxi drivers, and newsmen, and hotel clerks... anyone who would chat with him.

He wanted to know what they thought of Chrysler products, and Chrysler advertising. If they had a comment on the local Chrysler dealer, well, he was interested in that too. Where Diogenes went out looking for an honest man, Ron Todgham went out looking for some honest answers. I have always admired his approach.

Another memorable exchange with the top drawer occurred when I was at the *Brandon Sun*. I was on the committee that was arranging a large conference for farmers who were worried about rising interest rates. For a keynote speaker we needed someone of prominence in the world of finance. The name of Roly Frazee was mentioned, he was president of the Royal Bank. I was nominated to issue the invitation.

The local Royal Bank manager gave me the name of the president's secretary and her telephone number. As my experience with bank presidents is limited in the extreme, I made preparations for my pending chat. On a pad of foolscap I prepared my opening comments. When that secretary answered her telephone, I was going to be ready, aye ready.

I dialed the telephone. It rang. I waited for that female voice—and I didn't get it. Instead I heard a man's voice, and ever so briskly he said, "Good morning, this is Roly Frazee speaking!"

Well, there was nothing to do but laugh—which I did. I explained that I wasn't prepared to speak to him; rather, I wanted to chat with his close helper, who would do such things as check the presidential appointment book.

I was so impressed by our conversation that I can still recall most of it to mind. Mr. Frazee explained that he was everlastingly curious about all aspects of his bank and its public relations, and because of this he had developed a casual telephone-answering arrangement. Periodically, for a week at a time, he would answer all incoming calls. As in the case of Mr. Todgham of Chrysler, this was instructive.

What he learned was that, in many cases, if someone called the president's office and had a complaint, that complaint was sidetracked onto another executive just to keep bad news from the boss. No sidetracking is possible when the Big Cheese himself answers the telephone.

I have a strong feeling that today, with rare exceptions, we are living in a period marked by invisible executives. At a recent conference, this subject came up both directly and in an oblique manner. Several speakers told of the problem today of our world being directed by nameless, faceless individuals who sit in far-off places and make the big decisions that run our lives.

I think that's a pity. I want senior executives to be visible, to be vocal. I want them to have opinions, and to utter them. I say a real leader must have a public presence. I believe we should be able to get a message to them if we don't like what they're doing. If they collect executive compensation, I think they should hear from those of us who make this possible.

Horse Country

As I have told you several times, I am a serious collector. I collect small-town, small-scale enterprise stories. I am impressed by persons who make their own jobs.

The more of these case histories I collect, the more I become selective. I now have a special interest in those that were launched on a shoestring.

Well, Gail Campbell's enterprise certainly qualifies.

Gail is a farm homemaker from the Manitoba village of Cypress River. For a couple of years, after her marriage, she was on the staff of the *Treherne Times*, a weekly newspaper. This was great training: she learned to sell ads, take pictures, write copy, lay out pages—the works.

When she was on maternity leave, following the birth of her first daughter, she wished she had an income. She decided to put her training to work by combining it with her love of horses.

Her plan was to produce a periodical that would do for horses what the *Auto Trader* does for automobiles.

She contacted friends who had horses for sale and she sold her idea. She wrote profiles on the horses, and she took their pictures. She also collected her fee in advance. As she told me in our first interview, "I had zero capital. I had to collect that money in order to pay the printer."

That first edition of *Horse Country* was a modest effort: fifteen horse pictures and histories in eight pages. Gail Campbell mailed bulk packages of copies to tack shops, where they were given away. They were an instant hit.

In her second edition, she offered subscriptions for sale at $6 per year. As soon as she received her first six-dollar cheque, she realized she was hooked: now she had to produce more editions.

The second edition had some editorial copy in it, and gradually Gail developed her publication philosophy. Here are her words, right out of my notebook: "My plan was to provide a single source of information covering every aspect of the pleasure-horse industry: horses, saddles, trainers, shows, farriers, and feed stores."

Gail Campbell set the frequency of publication for *Horse Country,* at six weeks. For the first five years, she wrote every word of the copy. She has two computers for processing copy. She takes her own pictures, composes her own pages, and mails them to the printer in Steinbach.

Horse Country is a conspicuous success story. From that first eight-page edition six years ago, it has been through a remarkable transformation. The first edition published in 1996 had 136 pages, and went to 3,500 subscribers. Originally Gail served horse lovers in Manitoba only, but she now carries ads and stories from Saskatchewan, and has hired a representative in that province.

I chatted with her a while ago when Gail and her husband Tom were at the Royal Manitoba Winter Fair in Brandon. They gave me a copy of the current edition, which I read with interest.

Even to this non-horsey reader, this was informative copy. I didn't know, for example, the extent of the pleasure-horse industry. I certainly didn't know that Manitoba now has a horse crematorium. It is located at Headingley. Nor did I know that brothers Vern and Jeff Taylor had invented an electronic apparatus called FSA, which stands for Force Sensing Array.

Using this equipment, it is possible to measure how the saddle is pressing on the horse's back. If there is excessive pressure at some points, this will cause discomfort, perhaps even lesions over time.

Gail Campbell made me laugh when she told me that producing a periodical in your home, is something like having a monster in your closet. The reason she has no objections to this monster is that it is all hers; it is of her own design; it is a successful enterprise... and besides all of this, it has enabled her to be a stay-at-home Mom for her daughters, Bonnie and Kelly, ages six and eight, respectively.

The six-week publication cycle of *Horse Country* made it possible for Gail Campbell to fit her home-based monster into the domestic cycle in the household. She has made it mesh with the usual wifely responsibilities on a busy grain-and-cattle-farm.

The subscription rate has increased to $20. There now is money for pay for copy written by freelancers. Gail has hired a part-time typist.

Now that she has been going steady with a monster for close to six years, Gail Campbell has some fixed ideas on the world of work. "We spend the majority of our lives at work, so it only makes sense that we should spend that time doing something we like."

"In my case, I started my own business so I could stay home with my children. I work hard to balance my personal life with the demands of the business. I find that our lives flow around the production cycle of the paper, and the seasonal cycles of farming."

On The Banks Of The Birdtail

ONE EVENING AS I WAS SURFING AROUND THE INTERNET I SPOTTED the name of a favourite community, Birtle, Manitoba. This is a village of 840 located in the panoramic valley of the Bird Tail River.

Now, before I tell you my story, I will digress long enough to tell you about that name. Birtle was settled by Scots, who spoke English with a heavy oatmeal accent.

They couldn't say Bird Tail the way you and I do. They sort of gargled it so it sounded like "Baird-t'l." They did this so long and so often that the town that should be Bird Tail ended up as Birtle.

Anyway, I insist that some of the most handsome web pages on the Internet are those of Birtle, Manitoba. They are both attractive, and informative, and they invite you to respond to their offer of information. I responded by calling the telephone number they displayed.

My call was taken by a young volunteer, Angie Bray. When she isn't answering the telephone for what is called "Birtle Into The Future," Angie is a school teacher. Angie helped me fill a couple of pages in my notebook.

A year ago, two local residents, Brenda Evans and Kathy Langford, were strolling in their beautiful valley setting. It is reported that they simultaneously reached a major conclusion: Birtle's blessings should be shared with others. They began to devise a promotion program. They collected one thousand dollars each from the town, the rural municipality, and twelve hundred dollars from the Lions Club.

Their first project was an Open House, which included a wide variety of entertainment. They offered home-building lots for sale for $1 each. They also offered a red-hot deal on five empty buildings. Any company that started a small business in one of those buildings—and kept it going for five years—would be given the clear title.

They contracted for an 800 telephone number. They turned to the local computer wizard, Jeremy Geras, a grade-nine student. Youthful Jeremy is the designer of those beautiful web pages. Those web pages promote Birtle and its 800 number.

By this time I can hear you asking, what happened from all this activity?

Well, brace yourselves, for this is a remarkable story.

As of a month ago they had received 350 telephone calls. Three hundred of those callers wanted the informational package that was offered. One hundred and thirty callers actually visited Birtle. The major source of calls is British Columbia. They were made by persons who feel threatened by the west-coast cost of living.

A few persons put down a dollar for one of those building lots, but they did not build the required new homes. However: twelve families did buy older homes and they moved in. There's a small garment factory operating in one of those empty buildings. Emboldened by the success of their first venture, the Birtle-ites are planning for this year. Their first program is a summer camp for seniors, with a different activity for every day. Those who don't arrive with their own trailers will be billeted in local homes.

What I like about the Birtle promotion is its design. Everything is being done from within local resources, with a successful recipe: a good plan, a little money, a lot of volunteers, and a double helping of the prairie spirit.

Dryland Navy

Talk about a surprise. Wow!

I was halfway between downtown Winnipeg and the airport when I was stopped in traffic. I peered around, checking out the territory. On my right I saw a building that looked faintly familiar. Then I did a double-take when I saw the address over the door: 583 Ellice Avenue.

Well, a couple of eons ago this was the headquarters of HMCS Winnipeg. I checked in there as an ordinary seaman (extremely ordinary) right after the outbreak of World War Two. As part of the process I even surrendered my name. I became just #9695.

Every morning we did close-order drill. Every afternoon we went upstairs to learn the Morse code. For me this was duck soup; I had just checked out of my job at CPR Telegraphs.

At the end of the first month I was ordered to stand my first watch. It began at six p.m. on Saturday evening.

I reported for duty sharp on time. The officer of the watch stroked my name off the list, then asked me to follow him up to a part of the building I had never previously visited: the officers' mess.

My guide reached into a closet and took out a small strainer, the type my grandmother used when she was serving tea.

I was led to the bar. At either end were two large artillery casings. The tops were fitted with containers that held white sand. These were ashtrays.

I was instructed to sift this sand.

Now, you may be curious as to what was going on, and certainly I was. But, I also had a powerful motivation to do what I was told. After all, in the navy, Rule #1 for ordinary seamen is: "Don't ask questions... no matter what you're told to do—just do it!"

So, I sifted, still wondering what this was all about.

I found matches, and cigarette butts, and even the remains of a cigar or two. And then I came across a number of mysterious pellets I could not identify. At this point I had a strange sensation: something was rubbing up against my ankle.

I looked down. It was a cat. Not an ordinary cat, mind you, but one of a pair of pampered Persians that lived in the officers' mess.

CLICK! That's the sound of the light going on upstairs. Now I knew what I was doing: those ashtrays were also the comfort station for these blasted felines. I had just been promoted: I was now captain of the cat latrines.

As I sifted I reflected. I once had been certain that Hitler lost some sleep just as soon as he learned that I had enlisted. I wondered if he knew what I was doing right now to combat that submarine menace.

More memories.

I came out of 583 Ellice one afternoon and held the door for a young army officer who was entering. Another surprise. This was my officer, or so I thought.

I was in a small crew under the guidance of Lieutenant Dexter Ginn, whose family were furriers. If I had seen him at work all morning in a navy uniform, how come he could spend the afternoon in a uniform that was definitely army?

Well, this is easy if you have an identical twin. I was soon to learn that when the Ginn boys entered the services, Dexter went dark blue, brother Mac went khaki.

That same Lieutenant Dexter Ginn marched a bunch of us down Ellice Avenue one afternoon to the YMCA for our swimming trials. To pass, we had to swim two lengths of the Y pool, fully clothed. We could take off shoes and caps... nothing more.

Now, few of you can calculate the amount of water that can be soaked up by one sailor's heavy navy serge. My estimate is seven tons.

At the end of my first length I was puffing, and I had a serious complaint: my tunic was binding my shoulders and I couldn't take a complete stroke.

On the second length I had a more serious problem: I was running out of energy. I still have a flashback of Lieutenant Ginn standing at the end of the pool, urging me on. With half a length to go I almost said to heck with it, I'll just sink out of sight and let someone else win the war. But—I persevered. I'm still happy that pool wasn't six feet longer.

Another memory. A month later those of us in the first wave left Winnipeg, bound for Halifax on a special train—nothing but young sailors. Seeing me off was my uncle, Dr. Fred McGuinness, and his wife, my Aunt Eva. Aunt Eva gave me a wristwatch, and Uncle Fred gave me some sage advice.

He said that in the First War, he had learned how to get along in the services: "Keep your bowels open, and your mouth shut."

Well, at least I can say that I scored fifty per cent.

The Inspiring Duncan Callum

I KNOW A STORY WHICH MAY INSPIRE YOU... IT CERTAINLY DOES this to me.

This is the story of Duncan Callum. He resides in the Village of Miami, Manitoba. Duncan and his guide dog Mona are a daily sight on the streets of his home community.

When he was six, Duncan Callum was diagnosed as being diabetic. By the time he was 22, he was blind. At some point in the intervening years, he must have made up his mind that he was never going to let a disability hold him back.

Here's my favourite example of this man's spirit.

Roughly a year ago Duncan heard that the Village of Miami and nearby Town of Carman were being awarded a Community Access grant. The purpose of this money was to help the towns make a connection with the Internet.

Because he had been listening to informational cassettes distributed by Canadian National Institute for the Blind, Duncan knew that he could take a major advantage from the new, global medium.

He bought a computer. He also bought the instructional cassettes which taught him how to use it. He called on technically-trained friends to equip his computer with a voice synthesizer. As soon as the Internet connection was made, Duncan was one of the first persons to sign up for the new service.

Every evening now he starts up his computer and listens to the newspapers: the *Winnipeg Free Press*, the *Globe and Mail.*

This man, who never previously wrote a letter, now has e-mail correspondents by the score. Most of these keyboard buddies share interests with Duncan: either they are blind and are learning how to use computers; or they want to share experiences with their guide dogs.

Having interviewed Duncan Callum three or four times now, I am no longer surprised at his accomplishments. He has an office job; he's a clerk in the Miami office of Investors Group. Thanks to Braille, he does the filing. He also answers the telephone, looks after the banking and the mail.

He's the long-time coach of Miami's senior baseball team. I questioned him closely on this one, and he says it's not a problem. He's the one who makes up the batters' list, so he knows who is where. He says that listening to the crowd, and the umpire, he is able to tell what is going on in the field.

When his townsfolk decided to help him get a guide dog, they learned that the source of these talented animals is Lions International.

The next move was obvious: the Miami community formed its own Lions club, with Duncan Callum as one of the charter members. Fifteen years later he's still active. Twice he has been president, and next year he'll be president for the third time.

Every time I interviewed Duncan Callum I learned of another story that I found hard to believe. This man is not only an officer of the Miami Curling Club—he's also an active curler, with a regular spot on a club team.

He has worked out an arrangement with a team mate regarding the path his rock is to follow. He can't do the sweeping, and in replacement for this he holds the broom while his mates do the sweeping.

The guide dog, Mona, a black Labrador, is Duncan's third canine companion. For each of them he has made the trip to Rochester, Minnesota, for that 28-day training program in which a person with no sight meets his new companion. He admits that it is a challenge to be turned loose on the streets of a strange city with a dog whom you barely know.

But this is a man who loves challenges. That's why I find his accomplishments so inspiring.

Community Access

RECENTLY, I HAD A GREAT LEARNING EXPERIENCE.

Sixty of us convened recently at Portage la Prairie for a day-long meeting. In the audience were representatives of the 32 towns in Manitoba soon to make their connection with the Internet. They were successful applicants for matching grants provided by Industry Canada.

Those grants are made available through CAP—the Community Access Project. This is a federal response to rural depopulation. It is restricted to the smaller communities.

To qualify for a CAP grant a community must meet specific qualifications. There must be an established need. There must be dedicated volunteers. There must be an administration that will see the project through to the official opening. There must be evidence of a supporting network that will maintain this service in future years.

Communities that meet these requirements, become eligible for a one-time matching grant not to exceed $30,000. Industry Canada announced that 271 rural communities across Canada had qualified and would receive their grants.

This interesting experience at Portage la Prairie gave me a new respect for volunteerism. Those persons who are working on their small-town Internet connections must do the following things simultaneously:

- *Become knowledgeable in advanced electronics*
- *Recruit volunteers*
- *Raise money*
- *Train students, teachers, and librarians how to use this new medium*
- *Form those vital partnerships with merchants, doctors, lawyers, banks and credit unions, and health facilities, that will support and use the new connection in future years. Their support is critical: it costs money to keep each community network in business.*

I had a special reason for visiting with these interesting individuals.

I have a large writing project under way. Tentatively it is called: "The Internet in the Small Canadian Community." Recently, I have interviewed scores of individuals in small communities doing interesting things on the Internet.

I chatted with teenagers at Salmo Secondary School, in Salmo, B.C., who are engaged in a work experience with a clothing retailer, hundreds of miles away in Vancouver. They use the Internet for research; they interview other teenagers—literally around the world—about their likes and dislikes in present youth clothing styles.

I interviewed Peter and Paul Berry, of Eriksdale, Manitoba, who sell beef cattle and Boer goats via the Internet. The last time I spoke with them they had just sold some breeding stock to Nebraska, through this new medium.

A story from Cape Breton shows the influence of one talented person; Virginia Bergmann, a graphics artist and Internet fan, left Toronto to settle in the Village of Baddeck. Before long she had helped to create and establish 50 Cape Breton home pages on the Internet.

I have toured this unusual collection. You may buy craft works, or handmade stringed instruments, or bug-free shirts made especially for fishermen and woodworkers.

You may book hospitality at bed-and-breakfast homes.

The University College of Cape Breton promotes its distant-education courses.

Faith Baptist Church, in Sydney, reports that it regularly stuffs 242 adherents into the 200 seats in its sanctuary.

There's a home page on Ashley MacIsaac, and you should know who he is.

I'm a long way from being finished with my research into the Internet and the small town, but of this much I am assured: It is changing the lives and the economies of those small towns that now have access.

What the Internet does for the small town is banish distance: those old disadvantages of rural living are about to fly out the window, electronically, that is.

Anyway, congratulations to those small-town Internet volunteers. I know they face a daunting challenge, but think of the advantage they face: some day soon they, and their townsfolk, and the youngsters in the local school, will be connected to the greatest source of information in the world.

Enterprising Women

Here's a comment on a curious characteristic of the entrepreneur; ey're never quite content; never totally satisfied with their work.

As I see it, these self-employed persons are always questing for a slightly better way of doing whatever it is they do. I speak here from close observation.

Recently, at the 8th Annual Prairie Forum on Rural Development, in Saskatoon, I visited with three entrepreneurs about whom I have written for books or radio broadcasts.

In every instance, they had been through an evolutionary step. As I see it, once they get their venture operating in a satisfactory manner, they are always on the lookout for changes, improvements, new markets, perhaps even a new line of work.

Let me tell you about Maggie Mumm. She's a farmer who lives at Shellbrook. She and husband Jim are organic farmers who have a tiny specialty in the value-added world; they grow sprouting seeds. The next time you go through a smorgasbord line, and you see a bowl of sprouts, there's a good chance those seeds came from Hazelridge Farms, at Shellbrook, Saskatchewan.

Jim and Maggie are in their twelfth year as sprout-seed farmers. They have expanded their varieties to 36. They have expanded their market. It just delights me to think that a crew at work in tiny Shellbrook is filling packages with seeds the labels on which are printed in Chinese characters.

How come? Because the Mumms, who once sold only in North America, now have a major outlet in Taiwan. In a good year the Mumms will send more than 100,000 pounds of sprouting seeds to market. Much of that production goes to market in 100-gram packets.

Phyllis Threinen, of Dauphin, is the imaginative lady who designed the "Call Mom" telephone line. As a former counsellor, Phyllis knew there was a steady market for what she describes as "information of the type you will not find in the public library."

She installed a 900 telephone number in her home, and went into business. She sells information at a set price per minute.

What do people want to know? How can I live with a hyperactive child? Is my association with my teen-aged kids normal, or otherwise? How can I conduct a different kind of party for a 4-year-old, or even an 80-year-old? There are women, about to undergo a surgical procedure, who want to talk to someone who has personal knowledge of this operation. Phyllis finds these persons.

Phyllis Threinen is doing well with her "Call Mom" telephone line, but still she found time to design and publish a different type of book. She calls this one *The Internet Organizer.* It is a log book in which you can store all your e-mail addresses; details on your news groups; your world-wide web address list, along with a time log. This permits you to keep track of when you logged onto the Internet, and when you logged off.

The Internet Organizer is selling well. I anticipate that the next time I visit with Phyllis on the telephone she'll be into still another venture.

Number three of my interviews at Saskatoon was Patricia Birchall. This woman and a friend organized "Re-Wear," a company that makes what they call "Clothing with A History."

With a crew of 26 women, who work at home cottage-industry style, Patricia and her partner turn used denim and recycled buttons into caps, vests, skirts, even full-length dresses. Deal with Re-Wear and there is one thing of which you may be certain: you'll never see yourself coming down the street. Every item is original.

Patricia's new line is—how shall I put this?—unusual isn't quite strong enough.

She is the inventor of what she calls the "Skeeterbeater." This is a hat made of denim (natch), from the brim of which hang scores of pea-sized seeds. These seeds have been impregnated with a powerful repellent which was created for Patricia by the agriculture department, University of Saskatchewan.

I'll let you know how the "Skeeterbeater" works in its first field trial. I tried one on a week ago in Saskatoon, but it was 10 below, and mosquitoes were hard to find.

But back to my entrepreneurs. They're a restless bunch, never quite content with what it is they're doing. Perhaps right there is the reason they keep turning their hands to such interesting enterprises.

Michael Millar: A Man Who Cares

THERE IS A SUBSTANTIAL REASON WHY I BELIEVE IN SERENDIPITY: it works. Like today. Because I was searching for one story, I ended up with two of them. That's a serendipitous experience. Serendipity happens only to the earnest seeker.

Story number one has to do with a Saskatoon man name Michael Millar. A friend of mine explained that Michael was doing clearly remarkable work as administrator of the Saskatoon food bank. He has thousands of clients and he serves them well. But still he wants to do more.

This man has a strong belief that a number of individuals are being shortchanged because they have been denied the privileges known to the rest of us. He worried over food-bank clients who are illiterate. Rather than merely tolerate this unfortunate situation, he associated himself with a literacy program then in operation.

One day one of the teachers told him that some of the persons who had taken this training were now curious as to how they could have an introduction to the Internet. This reminded him of something of which he had often thought; he believed that there were many children of food-bank clients who were also being shortchanged because there were no computers in their homes.

When a representative of the Saskatoon freenet offered the foodbank an Internet connection, he jumped at it. Within a few weeks, and thanks to a donation of a computer donated by the Canadian Labor Congress, the food bank has an Internet connection, and it is busy.

For food-bank clients and their children who are not trained in Internet work—not to worry. At all times there are staff members and other volunteers on duty who will provide the necessary training.

Here's something I could never have known when I began this interview: This Michael Millar is the Michael Millar who played guitar and double bass for a musical group you heard about just a few years ago: Humphrey and the Dumptrucks.

Michael Millar and four friends, three of them fellow students at the University of Saskatchewan, made music for fun. Their special interest was folk music. Well, music for fun became a little more serious one summer at the Saskatoon summer fair when they were given an opportunity to conduct a folk festival.

At one point someone decided they should take all the participating musicians and have a jam session: as a gag, someone called this impromptu gathering, "Humphrey and the Dumptrucks." After the fair was over, and the five musicians decided to become more serious with their shared hobby, they decided this name was just silly enough to have show-business potential.

This was a great decision: this band lasted for 14 and one-half years. One of the original five had to drop out because of a family and a day job. Another decided to try his hand as a solo artist. But the other three played in every province and territory, save only Newfoundland. They travelled by van, and often clocked 60,000 miles per year, counting air travel.

Michael Millar has trouble adjusting for the differences between prices then, and prices now. When Humphrey and company first went on the road, they could move that van from Saskatoon to Vancouver for twenty dollars' worth of gas. In the late sixties, each man drew five dollars a day for food, and usually had money left over.

I asked Michael Millar if close to 15 years in show business had left him a rich man. He said yes, "Rich in experience."

When it was time to dissolve that folksy, blue-grass-type of troupe, Michael became a house-husband for a while, and then he worked for the musician's union. When he did this job he was a volunteer board member of the food bank. When the management position came open, he was asked to take it.

Michael Millar does not view managing a food bank as a job; rather it's almost a holy calling. He can't imagine doing anything else. He says his clients are nice ordinary people, just like you and me, who just happen to be down on their luck. It pleases him that he can be of service.

When he had an idea that perhaps the children of his clients should have a chance to become Internet proficient, he viewed this as nothing more than an extension of food-bank duties.

Anyone who manages a food bank must be able to adapt to changing situations. When a Hutterite colony offered the food bank a gift of potatoes—19 tons of potatoes—Michael's automatic response was "Send 'em over." He kept some for this own inventory, and parceled the rest out to other food banks. And there you have it: Two stories for the price of one. That's serendipity.

Observations On Teaching

I HAD OCCASION THIS MORNING TO DO A SPOT OF RESEARCH: I wanted to know what the great and the near-great have said over the years about "teachers," and "teaching."

What I learned is something less than inspiring; it's really a heavy load of cynicism.

In *Sarah Binks*, Paul Hiebert writes of a teacher who had the educator's peculiar genius for imparting knowledge without himself assimilating it.

When he wrote *The Apprenticeship of Duddy Kravetz*, Mordecai Richler observed, "He could have been a success at anything he wanted. Instead, he's devoted his life to teaching."

In his *Sunshine Sketches* Stephen Leacock reports that, "I took to school teaching as the only trade I could find that needed neither experience nor intellect."

I wish—publicly—to reject all that irony and I do so by giving you a quotation of my own: "After 15 years of teaching a single university course, I view it as one of the world's great learning experiences."

Every September I meet 30 Brandon University students to whom I teach "Introduction to the Media." While, reportedly, I am the lecturer, I am also learning from these interesting young persons.

What have I learned from 15 years in this unusual relationship?

That it is not easy—these days—to be a full-time student. When I compare today's students, with those I met in campus life 50 years ago, I see few comparisons.

In those good old days, university represented an almost full-time social life, with a dance or a skit night at least once each weekend. Few students then had jobs, or needed jobs.

Well, this is not the case today. Today I have students who are just barely sneaking by, month after month, on the earnings from three or more part-time arrangements.

As we came to the end of the recent term, I asked the students to write me a two-part letter. I asked them to describe what they were doing to pay for tuition, and board and room. In the second part I asked about their plans for a career.

Out of 28 students, (I lost a couple along the way) there are only a small handful who are fully supported by their parents. The remainder have one, or two, or even three part-time jobs.

What do they do?

Operate the scale at a landfill; dress windows in department stores; a number work in restaurants as cooks, waiters, waitresses, or cashiers.

There's a part-time disk jockey at a country radio station. There are lifeguards and swim instructors. There are three students who receive assistance from their First Nations bands, in return for which they will take their learning back to their home communities.

About those careers: four out of 28 believe they are headed directly to journalism, in print, or electronic, or the Aboriginal media.

Several students want to become teachers. One of them is studying sign language because she wants to work with children with disabilities. One young male has picked out the university at which he will get his MA in history; he even knows where he will apply for his Ph.D. training.

A young man has an opportunity to join a successful family business, but he has doubts about its suitability for him. One young woman wants to become a police officer. Another is headed directly to law school. While she says she needs the legal training, it is her ambition to use it for mediation, as an alternative to the courts.

Of great interest is the number of young women who say their lives have been changed due to volunteer work. The more they worked with the disabled and the disadvantaged the more they realized how much they wanted to become advocates for those at the lower end of the economic scale. Their first choice of graduate course is either psychology, or social work.

And there you have my report on one tiny sample of today's university students. For many of them, every waking hour is booked in advance: if they aren't in class, or a lab, or the library, they're holding down one of their part-time jobs.

They're a well-motivated lot. Perhaps this is the way it has to be when you have to work so hard to get what you want.

Dief The Chief

A WHILE BACK, ON THE CENTENNIAL OF THE BIRTH OF JOHN GEORGE Diefenbaker, I read all those news stories with special interest. I have several recollections of this unusual man.

The history books show that the Prairies have seen few of their sons—and, regrettably, none of their daughters—make their way to the office of prime minister. As I recall the record it includes: Arthur Meighen of Portage la Prairie; Joe Clark of High River, and Dief the Chief from Wakaw and Prince Albert. All were memorable; two for the brevity of their terms; the third for the double helping of controversy he gave us.

I met Mr. Diefenbaker for the first time in 1953. At that time I was with Saskatchewan's Jubilee Committee. In the company of committee member John Archer, later the president of the University of Regina, I visited Ottawa to talk to the Saskatchewan members of Parliament. We wanted them to know what our committee was doing, and how they could assist us with things like commemorative stamps and coins.

It was an interesting meeting: there were some great ones around that conference table. M.J. Coldwell was there; James Garfield Gardiner was there; and of course Mr. Diefenbaker. I still recall how immaculately he was attired, with about four inches of French cuff showing. That evening John and I watched from the gallery as he assailed the Opposition, reaching over his desk so far he almost stabbed them with his forefinger.

My jubilee training stood me in good stead, for a few years later Mr. Diefenbaker appointed me to the board of the Canadian Centennial Commission. If any of you want to read the record of what that commission accomplished, you can find it all laid out in Peter Aykroyd's excellent book, *The Anniversary Compulsion*, published by Dundurn Press.

Now, I must digress for a minute and tell you about our chief commissioner. This was the late John Fisher, at one time known as "Mr. Canada." In my book he was one of this nation's greatest orators and boosters.

John Fisher at one time was a senior member of the Diefenbaker office staff. He resigned in preparation for his elevation to the Senate—although that appointment never materialized. Instead, his former boss made him chief of the centennial. Forever after, Mr. Fisher smouldered over the fact he was not Senator Fisher.

In those days, the centennial commission had a board meeting every other Monday; one meeting would be in Ottawa; the next would be in one of the provincial capitals. As we travelled, I often sat with John Fisher and listened as he explained what things were like in the prime ministerial office.

Let's just call it chaos squared. As it was reported to me, the PM refused to make decisions, with the results that the staff members were barely this side of a collective anxiety attack.

Because of my curiosity about this subject, I was deeply interested when Peter Newman's book on Diefenbaker was published. It was called *Renegade in Power*, and for the first time I saw the Dief's quirk explained in detail.

It was the Newman thesis that Diefenbaker, who loved power, had a curious belief that every time he made a decision he diminished that power—hence he didn't make decisions. Peter Newman and I engaged in quite a correspondence on this subject.

I have another recollection of Diefenbaker and of his strange ability to show the human touch. He loved the Prince Albert constituency, for he was the third PM to hold it. Both Sir Wilfrid Laurier and MacKenzie King had used it as a convenience riding when they lost elections elsewhere. Prince

Albert National Park, with Waskesiu as its core, is just one of the benefactions P.A. received from all that prominence.

One day when Prime Minister Diefenbaker was going fishing, complete with aides and Mounties, he saw a young lad of about 10 standing on the dock, watching. The PM invited that boy to join him. Dief and Billy Brown, of Medicine Hat, spent the entire day together. Billy is the son of Medicine Hat lawyer W.Z. Brown.

Well, a year later the PM was to visit Medicine Hat and make a policy speech at the Arena. I was standing near the Arena door when the parade approached. I could see the PM seated on the back of a convertible.

A few yards away from the front door, Diefenbaker called "Stop the car." The car stopped. The PM got out of the vehicle, waded into the crowd, and put his arm around Billy Brown, who was watching from the sidewalk. Billy and the PM renewed acquaintances while the cameras clicked and onlookers had their curiosities working overtime.

I thought then—and I haven't changed my mind—how strange it is, that a man who really didn't know how to run a country, could reach into a crowd of hundreds and pick out the face of a lad he knew only casually, and had not seen for a year.

In case you wonder why we keep on talking about John George Diefenbaker, it's because—whatever he was doing—it was never ordinary. He was forever doing things which surprised us. Perhaps that's why we talk about him long after his death.

Dying, Death, And Funerals

IN CASE YOU BELIEVE I AM IN A SOLEMN MOOD TODAY—YOU ARE correct. Today the subject is dying, death and funerals.

This item began with a telephone call from a friend on the eastside of the province. A few weeks ago he went through a trying period: his mother was dying of cancer in one hospital; his father was dying of emphysema in another.

When their strength was up to it, these terribly ill persons would have a brief chat on the telephone. In one of these calls, the man said to his wife: "I think I shall die tomorrow. Do you think you'd like to die, too, so we could take this final trip together?"

The response was truly grandmotherly: "No. I'll not die tomorrow. I want to hang on long enough to know that our granddaughter's child is born safely... and then I'll go." And he died the day following, and grandmother died after she heard of the safe birth.

As I thought about this unusual conversation I reminded myself that in recent months I have had several reasons to write a "letter" on this subject.

In the past couple of years I have lost three friends for whom there were no funeral services. One was a boyhood chum, one was a lifelong friend of my family, and one was a former workmate. In all instances this lack of a funeral was their specific request, and their families honoured those wishes.

Now, I mention this today because that lack of a funeral service is something I find troubling. It's almost as if I can't close the file on that individual... it seems there's outstanding business. In the case of that boyhood chum, ever so willingly would I have crossed the continent to pay final respects, but this was not to be: no funeral.

Talk of funerals makes me think of a reporter with whom I once worked. His name was Harald Gunderson, and he was a man of noteworthy zeal. I can prove this. At Medicine Hat, the newspaper office was only a block from the fire hall. When the sirens wailed, I could look out my office window and see which way the wagons were going.

To my astonishment one afternoon, I looked out to see Harald Gunderson standing in the middle of the street, waving at an oncoming fire truck. That truck slowed down, and when it passed Harald, he grabbed hold of the railing at the back and swung himself on board. This was one fire at which he was going to be a close observer.

When he quit the newspaper, it was only to enter another form of journalism: He became publisher of a periodical called "World of Beef." I didn't hear from him for a number of years, and when we became re-acquainted, he then was publisher of a magazine called the *Canadian Funeral News*.

Well, friend Harald is now deeply immersed in the last rites. He wrote and published two large hard-covered books, *A History of Funeral Service in Alberta*, and *Funeral Service in British Columbia: A Century of Caring*.

Each of these books tells the story of funerals through the history of the individual funeral directors and their mortuaries. Some of the ancient pictures are remarkable. One is the funeral cortege for Sir James Lougheed, Calgary, in November of 1925.

There's another that might surprise you: the funeral of Sam McGee. I'm talking about that Sam McGee; Now, Sam McGee was from Tennessee, Where the cotton waves and blows... you know the rest of that one...

Contrary to what Robert Service would have you believe, Sam McGee spent his remaining years on his daughter's farm, near Beiseker. He suffered a stroke in 1940 and was buried in the yard of Rosebud Church. I have seen a picture of the crowd that gathered for the last rites.

Now, I mentioned at the outset that I was going to be solemn today, but that will be difficult from this point on: Funerals may not be cheery occasions, but you can find humour in some cemeteries.

Friend Harald Gunderson has spent a lot of time in cemeteries, observing and photographing the tombstones and their inscriptions: two are worthy of special note.

While I cannot even guess what went on in one certain household, I can tell you what the widow put on the grave marker:

GONE—BUT NOT FORGIVEN.

Another one that appeals to the commercial side of me reads:

HERE LIES JANE SMITH
WIFE OF THOMAS SMITH, MARBLE CUTTER
THIS MONUMENT WAS ERECTED BY HER HUSBAND
AS A TRIBUTE TO HER MEMORY AND AS
A SPECIMEN OF HIS WORK
MONUMENTS OF THIS SAME STYLE
THREE HUNDRED AND FIFTY DOLLARS.

The Witless And Wonderful Turkey

YES, WE HAD A TURKEY FOR THANKSGIVING; AND YES, EVERYONE enjoyed it, with only the turkey excepted.

As I carved this bird for a large, hungry, and attentive audience I had a major flashback to the spring and summer of 1974. That year I had a post-graduate course in the history of this witless and wonderful bird.

This story begins with a call from the editor of *Reader's Digest.* He got right to business: "Fred: we want you to write a story on the turkey."

At that time I was writing four or five features a year for that magazine, and I was game for almost any topic. But, turkey?

At this point it was explained to me why the turkey is so wonderful: no other creature in the world can convert feed with the same efficiency. If you want to produce a pound of beef, it will take eight pounds of feed; a pound of pork takes four. But nothing can match Melealgris Gallopavo, our domestic turkey. You give one of these birds two pounds of feed, you get one pound of flesh.

I say that's wonderful, but I also insist this bird is witless.

Turkeys will eat themselves to death. They will crowd into a corner of the fence and suffocate the ones on the bottom. They will drown in the watering trough. They will starve while facing a mountain of feed.

But they taste wonderful, and that's why they are so popular. They are also good for you; when it comes to protein, they rank next only to fish.

In the course of my research I visited the federal research station at Swift Current, where the turkey studies are carried out. At that time Dr. Ken Dunkelgod, the senior scientist, had a picture on his wall of the largest bird he had reared up to that point; 74 pounds. Try that one in your oven!

By the time I had finished visiting turkey farms, and eviscerating plants, and turkey-packing plants, I finished my story and turned it in. I thought that was the end.

Well, it wasn't. A month later I was asked if I would adapt the story for Reader's Digest U.S. edition. To do so I would have to get some copy from that country.

So, off I flew to the "Turkey Capital" of the U.S. of A: Willmar, Minnesota. I spent a couple of days with a producer named Huizenga, who at that time was raising nine MILLION turkeys each year.

One morning when he picked me up at the motel, Mr. Huizenga told me he had to do a little banking before we went on our tour. He asked me to join him.

Fascinating visit: As we walked into the bank, each clerk in turn got to their feet and called "Good Morning, Mr. Huizenga." This went on right down the line.

When we were back in his car I suggested he must be a prime customer to get service like that. He thought about his answer for a few seconds before putting it into words. Then he said, "A couple of years ago I had a smasher of a profit... so I bought the bank!"

Anyway, think about this when you are finishing off the carcass of that Thanksgiving bird: Turkeys are not known for their beauty; they may have been out of the room when the brains were being passed around; but no other creature can convert feed with the same efficiency.

In 1630, in Massachusetts, naturalist William Wood wrote: "The Turkey is a very large bird. He hath the use of his long legs so ready that he can runne as fast as a Dogge; and he can fly as well as a Goose."

Well, if William could see them now he would be in for a shock. A hundred generations later the turkey may or may not eat, may or may not breed, and it has lost the ability to fly.

But they taste so good we have made them our prime ceremonial bird.

Retirement

Report From Christmas Tree Farm

THIS IS A PROGRESS REPORT FROM CHRISTMAS TREE FARM.

It was motivated by an interesting after-dinner discussion. There were only two participants: Christine, my patient spouse of close to 51 years—and me.

After a treat of scalloped potatoes (one of my favourite dishes) and our daily game of Scrabble (I was trounced) Christine came up with a remarkable recollection.

She said it was exactly 22 years ago this week when we first set foot on the northwest corner of Section 17, township 10, range 19, west of the first meridian. Hereinafter known as Section 17.

On our first trip we ploughed through waist-deep snow in the roadside ditch: I held the strands of fence wire apart so Chris could climb through: we stared around at our 32 acres of horse pasture.

It was as bare as a pool table. The tallest thing in sight was some Russian thistle. We could not hear or see any wild creatures.

This was the first of many trips to our new property. Christine picked the location for the home, and set about designing it. I began to pace off areas for different purposes: shelterbelts here, orchard there, a garden in the middle flanked by a large (almost commercial in size) raspberry patch.

Nor can I forget a spot for the swimming pool. This quickly came to represent the most important part of our days from May to October. There's nothing like 50 laps to ease sore muscles after a hot day's work.

We had several reasons for moving to the country. I was only 10 years away from retirement, and obviously this called for some preparation. Three of our children had left the nest, and the fourth, Gallagher, was in the final boarding stages. As a student at UBC, he was home only during vacation periods.

I'd like to think we knew what we were doing. After all, we were deserting blacktop and civic utilities for gravel roads and a septic field. There was a lot of discussion involved here, but the decision was final and unanimous: we wanted to get away from city life. We wanted some new challenges, and we wanted more activities out of doors.

To settle our place in the country we became expert scroungers. When we heard of a home being replaced by a commercial building, we acquired truckloads of lilac bushes, and more truckloads of bricks for our patio. One morning, at a meeting at the International Peace Garden, I saw them ripping up a grove of ash trees for a road-building project. Gallagher and I were back there the next morning with our truck; all the ash trees we brought home survived.

With a tractor to haul the tree-planter, and three sons and one daughter, we planted tens of thousands of seedlings, mainly white spruce and scotch pine. This subject calls for amplification.

When you work on a tree planter you are sitting about four inches off the ground, immediately behind a back wheel of the tractor. There may not be a dirtier, dustier job in all of Christendom, but I don't know of another that's nearly as rewarding.

When those seedlings began to grow we were introduced to land reclamation. The land we now owned was classified was Grade 5 pasture. However, it would grow things, and with the tree growth came the wild creatures. Before long we had deer, foxes, coyotes and badgers on our land. It was obvious they liked what we were doing.

Country life also was an introduction to country characters, and some of the noteworthy talents you can find in the boonies. One of our neighbours, dairyman Walter Martinook, had been an aero-engine mechanic in the RCAF. If I were to call him, to ask if he had a quarter-inch bolt, three inches in length, with a fine thread and a hexagonal head, he'd say, "Come on over: If I don't have one, I'll make one for you."

It was interesting for a few years to operate a U-pick, U-cut Christmas-tree plantation. From the kitchen window Christine could see the cars and the patrons drive away. We learned the First Law of Christmas-tree sales: the smaller the car, the larger the tree tied on behind. Today we save the trees for the birds.

We produced honey, giving up this exercise in husbandry only when arthritis interfered. I may have been the only bee-keeper in Manitoba who made more money writing about it than I did from selling it. When visitors asked if the stings were bothersome, I had a standard answer: they're really no trouble at all, after the first hundred thousand.

Rural residents are forever watching the wildlife. We loved seeing the deer in the backyard. From May through to Labour Day we became ardent watchers of the songbirds.

Having lots of room for growing things, we always grow too much. All the shelves in the cold room are filled with jams, jellies and pickles. There are three freezers—also filled. It's a comfort having all this food. We really don't mind being snowed in, and, we're certainly ready for that unexpected load of visitors.

It was this business of reminiscing—nostalgia it is called—which kept us at the dining table last evening until we were chatting in the dark.

It is almost impossible to grasp all that has happened in those 22 years. A section of horse pasture has come to resemble a mini-forest. A country place has changed the lives of this aging couple, and certainly it has changed our schedules: in the winter we are rarely out; in the summer we are rarely in.

And there's my report. And now you must excuse us, for we have things to do—Christine is going to plant the peas and carrots; my job is to plant the potatoes.

Potatoes As Therapy

LET ME REPORT TWO SEPARATE, BUT LINKED ITEMS OF PERSONAL NEWS:

A: The kink has gone from my lower back.

B: The potatoes have been harvested and now are in the cold room.

I developed that kink digging and picking and sacking a large crop of spuds. No complaints, mind you, for this is a job I like, and a vegetable I really like.

And, it may surprise you to learn that during their growing period, potatoes can be a writer's best friend. Well, this writer anyway.

There are days on which my precious paragraphs are not working out just the way I want, and this calls for a break in the action. If it's summertime, I head for the workshop, pick up the hoe, and take off for the potato patch.

There is something about that delightful combination of sunshine, light exercise, and quietude broken only by birdsong that helps me sort out that problem I'm having with the words.

There's another reason I like potatoes; I have written about them for a number of magazines and newspapers. In recent years they have become a major item in the Manitoba farm economy. The announcement that another $50 million will be spent to enlarge the Manitoba potato-processing industry is of major significance.

There is one aspect of this industry that interests me more than all the rest; it has to do with the processing plant at Carberry, where 600 employees turn out french fries for the four western provinces and many major cities in the U.S.

This story begins 27 years ago. The provincial agricultural representative at Carberry had a favourite saying, which he repeated endlessly, "WE'VE GOT TO GET TOGETHER TO FIND

OUT WHAT WE CAN DO TOGETHER—WHAT WE CAN GROW TOGETHER—WHAT WE CAN SELL TOGETHER."

That ag-rep was Welland Stonehouse. In 1974 he began working with five farmers who wanted to grow something other than grain.

Stonehouse directed these volunteers as they grew carrots on a research basis—and these were not a big success; nor were onions the year later; nor corn.

But they found a remarkable promise with potatoes. They not only began growing them on a commercial basis, but they raised $60,000 to buy land and hangars left over from the British Commonwealth Air Training Plan. This gave them potato storage.

They raised more money for the washing, grading, and bagging facilities. They incorporated under the name of Carberry Farms. Their venture had such promise that it attracted the attention of the major investor, J.R. Simplot. He bought them out. Within a few years scores of local farmers had potato contracts, and scores of millions were invested in a processing plant.

The co-operation that launched this potato industry in Carberry took other forms as well.

When the citizens decided they needed a major community centre, they spread the word around among the potato farmers. As a collective they got a potato contract. As individuals, each of them donated a few acres of land for potato production, with the proceeds going towards that hall. Every year this mini-co-op raised another $40,000 net towards that community hall.

Today at Carberry, potatoes are a multi-million-dollar industry, and it's there because leadership, and four or five farmers, meeting around a kitchen table, decided to try something venturesome.

Right there you find the prairie spirit at work...

Distinctive Communities

ATTENTION ALL RURAL RESIDENTS.

Here's a question for every reeve, mayor, councillor and rural activist: Is there anything that's really distinctive about your community?

Let me quote Oxford: to be "distinctive" means that you are distinguishing your community in order to make it different from all other communities.

This is not a casual inquiry. With every community interested in tourism, to be distinctive is a current widespread ambition. A growing number of communities are undertaking projects designed to attract attention to themselves.

One popular means of doing so is to erect a giant symbol in a prominent location. A dozen times every year—at least—the residents of a Manitoba community will hold a big discussion about what it is that makes them unique. With this settled, they then roll up their collective sleeves, get out their tin cups, raise some money, and place an order with a design house.

What are some symbols of distinction? How about the bull at Russell which promotes Beef and Barley Days, a local celebration of note? How about that statue of a Viking at Gimli which draws attention to the dominant ethnic strain? How about Killarney where you can see a statue of a leprechaun astride a frog?

If something happened in your community which clearly sets you apart from the rest of the world, that's your element of uniqueness. Certainly this is the story at Dominion City, nearby which Sandy Waddell used an axe to slay the largest fish every taken from Manitoba waters. It was a 400-pound sturgeon which measured 15 feet, six inches. He needed a team to haul it home. It now is memorialized in a life-size statue. (Don't scoff: I have a picture of that sturgeon.)

Roseisle plays on the community name with a 12-foot rose-bush. Local welder and ironworks designer Cliff McPherson, with the assistance of his wife Vickie, fabricated each petal, leaf, and thorn. At Lynn Lake they built the world's largest comic strip as a salute to local artist, Lynn Johnston, creator of the comic strip, "For Better Or Worse."

Some communities will do anything for publicity. Boissevain once offered $1,000 to the first female to climb to the top of their 25-foot turtle without the use of ropes of ladders. I have a picture of Janice Freeman perched on top of this symbol, but she won't say how she got there. Skullduggery is suspected.

Not all symbol suggestions win instant favour. When someone said a hog could represent Neepawa, home of a major pork-processing plant, *Neepawa Press* editor Jack Gibson said, "In a pig's eye." What friend Jack didn't know is that at Englefeld, SK, there's a 15-foot, 800-pound pink pig which symbolizes their major annual event: the combination home-coming-hogfest. With the tourists, it's a winner, or should that be wiener.

Flin Flon has Flintabbety Flonatin, after whom the town was named. Virden has an oil derrick. Selkirk has a catfish. Meleb has a mushroom. Grunthal has a buffalo. Poplarfield has a deer. Glenboro has a camel. Onanole has an elk. Roland has a pumpkin. St. Claude has the largest smoking pipe in the world... and it really smokes.

Just because you come up with a great idea, doesn't always mean that the neighbours will adore it. Take Komarno. When it erected a giant mosquito, in honour of a local specialty, the community boosters at nearby Teulon threatened to erect a 15-foot can of Raid.

Symbols must be maintained. When a windstorm took the head off Lundar's symbolic goose, local residents decided to have the whole statue replaced with a more durable model.

At Inwood, those famed garter-snake pits are honoured by statues of a king-sized pair lovingly entwined. On the assumption that snakes stutter, the local wags call the female S-Sarah, while her boyfriend is S-Sam. They are made of fibreglass, polyurethane, steel and mesh. Price: $13,000.

And, if you want to be more distinctive than all those other distinctive communities, do what Oak Lake did: get a symbol that lives and breathes. Arguably the most popular living thing in Oak Lake at this moment is Isaac, the ox. What he symbolizes is the historic fact that Oak Lake for years has been home of the world's largest Red River cart.

This is not a complete list, nor do I know if one of these exists. All I know is that I view each symbol as good news; each of them reveals to me that the local residents took an initiative designed to make their hometown distinctive. I say that's the prairie spirit at work.

Conrad Black And Me

As I see it, there isn't room for both Conrad Black and me in Southam Incorporated: one of us will have to go.

Mr. Black wants me to surrender my 32 shares. On the other hand, I insist that they are vital to my well-being. My holding may be minuscule, but those shares are important. They keep me on the corporate rolls. They permit me to receive quarterly reports, annual reports... even daily news on share value. Those shares make me a participant in the unfolding revolution in the Canadian media.

There is also the matter of pride of ownership: They are all mine and they are all paid for.

Because my corporate interest is so small, it brings distress to the transfer agent. After all, it costs money to look after mini-holdings, like mine. They have the expense of sending me dividend cheques, some of which total all of $1.60.

Regularly I receive these begging letters, imploring me to sell out. In turn, I ignore all these entreaties. I intend to stay.

The roots of this story are planted deep in the year 1958. Southam's then-president, St. Clair Balfour, called me at the *Medicine Hat News*, and told me he had a job for me to do at Southam's annual meeting: I was to be a scrutineer. I was to keep track of the number of shares that were being voted by each shareholder. Just before he hung up he also said that, to fulfill this assignment, I should be a shareholder.

Well, I checked with the local broker. Southam shares at that time were worth $63. Putting together all available cash, I really plunged and bought two.

At this point I must digress. Those of you with good memories may remember the exploits of "One-Share" Sweeney. In an earlier period, this man was the scourge of the giant corporations: he would buy a single share in a major company, which entitled him to attend the annual meeting. There, he would harass the president about his income, and the size of his expense account.

Well, I was twice as important as "One-Share" Sweeney: I was "Two-Share" McGuinness. I reported for duty.

One of my first customers was a tall, dignified gentleman who introduced himself as G. Hamilton Southam. In my boyish ignorance I asked him if he was a shareholder. He said yes. I said how many shares do you own: he said... brace yourselves... sixty-eight thousand. I did a quick calculation of their value—it was in the millions. I decided to let him in.

Here's another digression, and it concerns a recent news story. One of Mr. Black's associates said that from now on, he hoped that Southam publishers would operate in an autonomous manner, motivated by nothing more than the good of their communities.

This story really interested me, after all, I was employed by Southam when that company's executives wrote the book on the autonomy of the publisher.

It is hardly an exaggeration to say that in the '50s and '60s, a Southam publisher was a corporate baron, and the company property was his private fiefdom.

In the first week in which I was publisher of the *Medicine Hat News*, I received a letter from Britton Osler, a member of the executive committee. He welcomed me on board, and then he told me two things I could not do: change the insurance, or change the banking arrangement. Apart from these injunctions, I was encouraged to manage the asset as if I owned all the shares.

When President Balfour made his first trip to see me, I had a list of 23 questions which had arisen in the first four months of my new responsibility. One by one I read them out, and each time I did, Mr. Balfour said, "That's a local matter... YOU must answer that one."

I put my autonomy to the acid test when I needed a new editor. Twice in as many years I turned to old friends from the Winnipeg Press Club. Both Garth Hopkins and Bill MacPherson were in the editorial department of the *Winnipeg Tribune*, another Southam division.

Editor-in-chief Carlyle Allison wrote a letter to the president, complaining that I was stealing his key personnel. I thought that when it comes to autonomy, the reply was a classic: Allison was told to get busy and steal them back.

If you have been listening closely, you may have noticed that I described my Southam share holdings in two different ways: at one point I mentioned two shares, and at another thirty-two.

Well, that's called corporate success. When Southam practiced local autonomy for the publishers, the results were rewarding—literally. When the price went up, my shares were split, and two became four, which became eight, then sixteen... and then thirty-two.

It's about time for another letter from Royal Trust, begging me to surrender my shares. Next time I shall reply with the suggestion that they stop harassing me, and instead buy back fifteen or twenty million shares from Mr. Black.

As for me, I'm staying.

The So-called Gentle Sex

IT COULD BE DENIED NO LONGER: THE DRIVEWAY HERE AT CHRISTMAS Tree Farm required a load of gravel. I called the supplier. He said the delivery would be made at eleven o'clock on Saturday morning.

As forecasts go, this was a great one. At exactly eleven a huge dump truck came thundering down the municipal road and turned in to our place. There was only one surprise: at the wheel was a slender young women. We chatted briefly about how we wanted the gravel spread, and then she went to the back of the vehicle to attend to the tailgate. Varoom, and away she went, all 16 wheels hard at work. The job was soon done.

This set me to thinking about the changes in social custom. At my age—on a clear day—you can see a long way back. In my boyhood, I had one friend whose mother left the home each morning and went to work. She was a dentist's assistant; and she was a widow. Those were the days when the female teacher who had the nerve to get married also got drummed out of the service as if she had somehow disgraced the regiment.

When I became a telegraph operator in the Winnipeg office of CPR, I was surprised at the number of females also in the dot-and-dash business. Without exception they shared a common background; they were daughters of station agents in those days when every country railway depot had attached living quarters. These women grew up in an atmosphere of Morse code.

During the war, when I was sailing around Newfoundland and the Magdalene Islands—Grand Banks territory—I heard of women who were captains of fishing schooners, although I never met one.

During the harvest period on the Prairies I know in great detail what the homemakers can do: they can drive tractors, swathers, and combines. More frequently they drive those five-ton trucks that take the grain from the combine to the granary. In every way they were equal partners on the farm.

I have interviewed female carpenters and cabinet makers, although I have never interviewed a female plumber. I once flew from Brandon to Winnipeg on an airline that had a young female as a co-pilot. I know of female morticians. In a country rink last winter I saw a young female driving the Zamboni. In a Brandon machine shop called Atom-Jet, there's a young female who is a specialty welder: she puts the tips on cultivator shovels, what we once called plow shares.

In my student days I had a classmate named Donna Cruikshank. She wanted to be a doctor, but her father, in the spirit of the times, insisted that only boys were doctors, girls were nurses. But he did relent in one respect: if she would complete her nursing training, and still wanted to be a doctor, he would help her.

She did and he did. She retired a couple of years ago from Deer Lodge Hospital in Winnipeg as Dr. Donna Friesen. Friend Donna was the only nurse-doctor I ever met.

A few years ago, those of us in harness at the *Brandon Sun*, were surprised to realize that Brandon now had eight—count 'em, eight female lawyers in town. After all, Brandon went through its first century without one of these, and now we were replete.

Nothing would do but I interview all eight for a full-page feature. Here were more surprises. Four of that eight had had first careers as social workers. They had a common complaint: they could take a file only so far, and then they had to turn it over to a lawyer. This motivated them into a second career as lawyers. One of them now graces the bench.

This experience with females in the professions raised my curiosity and I called some deans at the University of Manitoba. There I learned that 40 per cent of the students in law were female, and sixty per cent of the students in pharmacy were female. Later I learned that of the 22 universities in Canada that provide training in journalism, 65 per cent of the students are female.

Do we still have some ancient taboos held over from yesteryear? Indeed we do. I have never seen a female locomotive engineer, or a female underground miner.

There is the occasional female with advanced training who yearns for a different line of work. Over a number of years I conducted one-day writing courses for the extension department of Brandon University.

One winter, in one of these classes, there was a young woman keenly interested in this business of scribbling. I know this because she asked many questions, and they were good ones.

A couple of months later, the class was repeated, and she appeared once again in the front row. When this happened three times in succession I finally had to ask her about her motivation.

She said she had a good job, but she needed a different one. I asked her what she did. She never gave me the name of the occupation, but she gave me a precise description. She said she spent every day with her right arm up a cow's rear end.

From this exchange I learned that, while being an artificial insemination technician is a skilled trade, it does have a few drawbacks. By the way, she now works full time for horse and rodeo publications.

All of the above leaves me convinced that we're not quite liberated as yet, but we certainly are heading in that direction.

They Shall Not Grow Old

THIS IS THE STORY OF A BOOK THAT IS LIKE NO OTHER. IT HAS AN unusual title: *They Shall Grow Not Old*. You should know this line: it's from *In Flander's Fields*, which you likely learned in elementary school.

This publication is truly unique. There is no other single reference available in which you can find the service biographies of the 18,000 members of the RCAF who lost their lives in WW2.

To assemble the material for this book, two men carried volunteerism to the ultimate. Les Allison, a retired farmer and an RCAF veteran, is an indefatigable collector of the memorabilia of war. Harry Hayward is a retired administrator for Manitoba Telephones. Harry was too young to be in service, but, like Allison, he is one of the many volunteers for Brandon's Commonwealth Air Training Plan Museum.

For Les Allison to collect this material was an heroic task: Canada's war dead are buried in over 70 different countries—but he did it over a period of years. Eventually he reached that point at which millions of bits of data had to be recorded in a computer.

His partner Harry Hayward, volunteered to do this, and I can only guess he didn't know what he was getting into.

This man is familiar with a computer that fills an entire room, and can handle thousands of telephone calls at the same time. In this instance, however, he had to deal with a single keyboard, and a small old-fashioned computer, and what is more, he had never learned to type. He began this giant task typing with one finger and eventually made the quantum leap to...two fingers.

To assemble the material for *They Shall Grow Not Old* these meneach worked five hours per day for eight years. When they finished, the book was published by the Commonwealth

Air Training Plan Museum. It was volunteers from this institution who raised the more than $90,000 to pay the printer.

Shortly after publication date I sat down with Allison and Hayward and they pointed out some of the case histories which touched them deeply. What I soon learned is that this is more, much more, than just a list of names and dates. There are deeply moving stories in these pages.

Most touching of all? The record of the deaths of Warrant Officer Russell Charles Smith, of Kamsack, SK, and Warrant Officer Howard Pilmore Low, of Vancouver. They were captured by the Japanese in the Far East. They escaped from the prisoner-of-war camp in Batavia, and made their way to the Kamarjan aerodrome. They managed to get into an aircraft, and had one engine going before they were recaptured. They died in front of a firing squad. In this book you can read the story of the Tod twins, Richard and Robert, of Winnipeg. They enlisted together, trained together, were assigned to the same air crew, and died together when their plane failed to return from operations over Europe.

There is the story of a brother-sister team who died in the same crash. Corporal Nora Johnson, was a meteorological observer, and her brother, Corporal Norman Johnson, was a member of a bomber reconnaissance squadron. They lost their lives when their plane crashed in British Columbia, killing all 14 RCAF members on board.

The heart grows heavy when you read stories like that of the Anderson brothers of Craigmyle, Alberta. Flying Officer W.B. Anderson was pilot of a Hudson aircraft which failed to return from an anti-submarine patrol over the Bay of Biscay. Flight Sergeant L.G. Anderson died in a raid over Nuremberg. Sergeant James S. Anderson died when the Halifax bomber in which he was an observer crashed in a three-engine landing in Yorkshire. In the record of all these deaths there are reminders that human kindness still exists. You find one such case in the entry for Flight Sergeant C.W.W. Peck, of Port Arthur,

Ontario, who lost his life when the Lancaster in which he was air gunner was shot down near Champignol, France. Peck was the only Canadian in the crew.

Half a century after Flight Sergeant Peck and his four comrades were buried in the cemetery at Champignol, the villagers are still placing fresh flowers on their graves.

After thanking Les Allison and Harry Hayward for the guided tour through their book, I pursued a private interest. I will read it to you as an example of a typical entry.

This is the service record of a brother-in-law I never knew; he was killed in action before I met my wife-to-be.

Here is what I read: "THOMSON, William Nairne, S/L (p) J-3254, from Port Arthur. Killed in action, Oct. 22/43, age 23, #434 Bluenose Squadron (In Excelsis Vincinus). Flew Halifax aircraft #LK663. Went down near Godelheim, Germany, during night trip to Kassel, Germany.

"There were 3, #434 Squadron aircraft lost in the same area on this date. S/L Thomson was buried in the parish cemetery at Godelheim, Germany, exhumed and reburied in the Limmer British Cemetery at Hanover, Germany."

One last word about Les Allison and Harry Hayward. Shortly after the publication of *They Shall Grow Not Old*, it was unveiled at an RCAF reunion. One man who spent considerable time thumbing through the pages made a discovery that should make us all pacifists: at war's end, he was one of only three survivors of his "wings" class of 50.

It happens, all too frequently, that you can read news articles in which commentators talk about the cost of war in dollars, dollars spent for tanks, and ships, and aircraft.

All too seldom do we read about those tens of thousands of young Canadians cut down in the prime of their health and intellect. Only a book like *They Shall Grow Not Old* can explain the cost of war in human terms.

Putting People On The Plains

ON THE EVENING OF NOVEMBER 25, 1896, THE MEMBER OF Parliament for Brandon arrived on the CPR train and a crowd of hundreds was waiting for him. His name was Clifford Sifton, and he was a brand-new member of the Laurier cabinet.

When Sifton stepped down from the train, a torchlight parade led him to the city hall, where the mayor was waiting in the council chamber.

Two days later, November 27, Sifton made a speech that created headlines. He announced his plan for a massive immigration program that would fill the Prairies with farm families.

Now, in that speech, Sifton made some comments which must have been viewed as hyperbole: he said he would cut through all the red tape in the immigration department, which reportedly had the reddest tape of all.

He said he would induce settlers with promises of free land. This too was interesting: the land in question was owned by CPR and Hudson Bay Company.

He said one thing more that I must admit I like: he was going to offer his staff a performance bonus. They would get extra pay for every new citizen they recruited for Canada.

While these were bold words from a brand-new member of the cabinet, you must consider them in light of the man himself.

This was a redoubtable battler: all he ever asked for was total surrender.

The Sifton motto was: "Never explain... never apologize."

Pierre Berton once wrote that Sifton had a mind like a steel trap, the memory of an elephant, and the hide of a rhinoceros.

Once Sifton got back to Ottawa, he needed these characteristics, because he had major impediments in his path. One was the deputy minister of immigration; the other the deputy in the Indian Affairs Department. There was a lot of heavy betting that Sifton could not remove these two men from office, but those who bet against the Brandon MP may not have known the whole story: Laurier had given Sifton all the power Sifton needed. Those deputies were fired.

It was at this point where Brandon's role in the settlement of the West took positive shape. Sifton hired Brandon's first mayor, Mayne Daly, to be the head of his legal department.

He hired Brandon's second mayor, James Smart, to replace both of those deputy ministers who had been ousted. He hired Will White, the publisher of the *Brandon Sun*, to be his director of press relations in the United States. Supported by what was called the Brandon team, Sifton went to work.

He flooded Europe and the U.S. with literature, and every word was carefully selected. The prairie winter climate was described as "bracing" and "invigorating." He once tried—unsuccessfully—to have Winnipeg's winter-time temperatures omitted from the weather reports.

The Sifton program worked. Within a year, settlers were arriving by the hundreds of thousands. And, just in case you think Sifton had an open-door policy, perhaps you'd like to re-think that ideal situation. It was specified that no "Asians, Jews, or Negroes" would be welcome on the grounds that they were not likely to become good farmers. This was not the age of enlightenment.

In the U.S., Will White was having great success in that nation, provided all the prospective Canadians had white skins. In 10 years, 217,000 American-born immigrants arrived on the Prairies, a few to Manitoba, a few more to Saskatchewan, and the bulk of them to Alberta.

While the eastern Prairies were settled by homesteaders who arrived with little more than the clothes on their backs, those American settlers were the sons and daughters of settled families in Iowa, Nebraska and the Dakotas. They arrived with boxcar-loads of possessions. By the way, one of Will White's immigration agents received a bonus of $3 for every one of those settlers.

Clifford Sifton—later Sir Clifford—did not last long in government, but while he was there he transformed a nation.

It is not an over-statement to say that he filled the Prairies with farm families, right from the Red River to the Rockies.

The Spirit Of The RCAF

IN MY WRITING CAREER I HAVE LONG FAVOURED PERSONAL STORIES, those which exemplify the human spirit.

It is not easy to describe the spirit, save to say that it is the animating force. Individuals who have spirit in abundance are certain to make more accomplishments in their lives than those who don't have it or—worse—who have it but won't turn it loose.

There's a powerful reason I have the spirit in mind today; I have just finished reading *Memories On Parade*, the personal recollections of a hundred or more RCAF flyers during World War Two.

This is not a continuing story as related by a single narrator.

Rather, this book has one-hundred-and-thirty-three authors, each of whom was a member of the air crew. These men responded—with feeling—when the Wartime Pilots' and Observers' Association asked them for a brief description of one particularly memorable wartime experience.

As you would expect, there are wide variations both in content and style. Each article—they range from five hundred to eight hundred words—is accompanied by a then-and-now picture of the writer.

With all of that as an introduction, let me tell you about the human spirit; it shines through in every story.

In October of 1940 the Warren twins—identical twins—joined the RCAF in Edmonton. Their names were Bruce and Douglas. Douglas writes this story.

When the Warren twins were awarded their wings, Bruce stood eighth in the class; Doug stood ninth. The first eight were awarded commissions. This left Bruce as a commissioned officer; and Doug as a sergeant. Let me tell you about brotherly love: Bruce applied to be de-commissioned so that he would be his brother's equal, but this request was lost in the paper war.

On shipboard, en route to England, Bruce had a stateroom up top, and Doug had a hammock in steerage—for a while, that is. Here's where the spirit comes in. Doug sneaked up to Bruce's stateroom and stayed there for the sea voyage. At meal time, Bruce would put on his pilot officer's uniform and go and eat, and when he came back, Doug would put on that same uniform and enjoy the treats in the officers' mess.

For their success as fighter pilots, each Warren twin won the Distinguished Flying Cross. They were presented by King George VI, who said this was an historic occasion; first time he had pinned identical medals on identical twins.

Another story I really enjoyed was that of Lou Crowe, a fly-boy who was vertically challenged. This may have been the shortest pilot in World War Two. At least if he wasn't, he says he never met anyone shorter than his own five-foot, one inch and a little bit.

Now, this was not a laughing matter. Every station on which Crowe trained had at least one instructor who gave him a "doubtful" rating. They doubted he would be a success as a pilot, because he might have trouble reaching the aircraft foot pedals. In fact, pilot Crowe had no trouble at all... as long as he had his pillow in the middle of his back. At a couple of stations, air-traffic controllers thought they had spotted run-away planes, but this was not the case: that was pilot Crowe taking off... they just couldn't see his head about the edge of the window.

Now, I must not let you think that this is all good fun and hi-jinks. While there is some humour, there's also heroism, and tragedy, and the problems of flying in machines that some times simply did not want to work.

Here's a bulletin from the small world department. Pilot William Carter had his plane badly shot up in an aerial battle, and he crashed into a house on the outskirts of a landing field.

Twenty years later he was back in England and he went to the scene of that crash. After he introduced himself, the homeowner went to a shed in the backyard and re-appeared bearing the propeller of that crippled plane. It now graces the Carter mantelpiece.

It is not possible to read these stories without reflecting on the extraordinary adaptability of youth.

The majority of these pilots joined the air force right after high school. Within a year many of them were in England, flying aircraft with which they had the bare minimum of training. It is little wonder that 50 years later their war-time memories are so clearly etched on their minds.

It happens on occasion that I will skim a book if the author doesn't command my attention, but this did not happen with *Memories On Parade.* I read every word, and may even read it all again.

The Last Letter

THIS IS A DAY I THOUGHT WOULD NEVER HAPPEN.

This is a day I could never have foreseen. I just assumed that Peter Gzowski and *Morningside* would keep rolling along just like the Assiniboine River.

Well, this is not the case. We have reached that point at which we must part.

This raises the question: how does one effect a parting after 12 or more years without becoming maudlin.

Lord Byron had one answer. In *Don Juan* he declared that all farewells must be sudden. If I believed that, I would be denied an opportunity to say what I am thinking.

I have been in the writing business for half a century. In this period I have had many assignments, but never one like *Morningside.*

Every week, as I made notes about my next assignment for Peter and Company, I would reflect that there isn't quite another program like this one. *Morningside* covers our favourite nation from Atlantic to Pacific to Arctic and all those points in between.

It was in the mid-'80s when I received a call from a senior *Morningside* producer. He said he wanted to chat. I asked what about. He said it didn't really matter because he just wanted to learn if I had a voice for radio. Then he asked me for my opinions on a range of subjects, and that was the end of that conversation. A couple of weeks later I participated in my first *Manitoba Report.*

Every other Monday morning I had to rouse myself at 5:30 to be in the Brandon studio on time one hour later. As a country-dweller it wasn't always easy to get there. On several occasions I had to put the accelerator to the floor to get through snowdrifts either on our road, or the municipal road.

There were technical problems. In those days I was expected to set up the equipment myself, following written-out orders. I could follow them too, only technicians kept making amendments to the equipment without telling me. In a couple of instances I could hear Toronto calling "Fred, Fred... are you there?" But they couldn't hear me.

They put in a security system without letting me know. I learned about this the hard way: I was just setting up the switchboard one morning when a Brandon city policemen came charging in, thinking he had interrupted a robbery in process.

I once kept all of my *Morningside* notes in a file folder, on the cover of which I wrote the name and telephone number of my Toronto contact. This document became a proof of the burnout in that busy office, because it contained literally scores of names.

It was three or four years ago when I said that perhaps the *Manitoba Report* should be passed on to younger hands, and this took me into a new phase of radio: the Letters Department.

Thanks to the firm but gentle guidance of Shelley Ambrose I became a Letter writer. My assignment was to say anything I wished as long as it wasn't a political editorial.

As I felt our relationship might continue over time, I asked Producer Ambrose how she wished to be addressed: Was she Ms? or Miss? or Mrs.? or just plain Shelley? None of the above she said. She had always fancied the title of Countess, and Countess Ambrose she became.

I soon learned that the radio listeners will always let you know what they like—and don't like. At least this is what happened to me.

They like people stories that are warm, perhaps humorous, perhaps uplifting. There is a strong preference for nostalgia. This was good news for me, because looking backward is one of my favourite sports.

Really, there was only one detrimental aspect to the Letters assignment: it took me away from direct contact with that gentle genius who runs the show.

There is no other way to describe Peter Gzowski's principal characteristics: he is a genius at his particular job. He evokes a flow of comment, both fact and opinion, from the interviewee, without ever insinuating his own opinions into the conversation. Whomever he was interviewing was the most important person in the world, and he let them carry the show without interference.

As a listener to *Morningside* I have come to view it as a sort of electronic magazine. I salute it for telling me many things about Canada I could find in no other medium. If our politicians have difficulty solving the problems of Canadian unity, let them finance more shows like *Morningside.*

It is time to say farewell: to Peter, to the Countess, to Linda and Gloria and Tom and many other telephone buddies, I wish you well.

I leave you with the thought of my partner Christine, a *Morningside* listener of note. In her opinion, it was a noteworthy decision to replace both the *Morningside* name, and the theme music. Let the new show stand on its own, freed of the curse of comparison.

The time has come for me to saddle up and ride off into the sunset. As I do, I shall look back with affection on a most remarkable experience.